Service Excellence

Service Excellence

Creating Customer Experiences that Build Relationships

Ruth N. Bolton

Service Excellence: Creating Customer Experiences that Build Relationships

The Center for Services Leadership (CSL) is a research center within the W. P. Carey School of Business at Arizona State University (ASU) and an outreach arm from ASU to the business community and the global academic community. The CSL has established itself as a globally recognized authority on how to compete strategically through the profitable use of services.

First published in 2016 by
Business Expert Press, LLC
222 East 46th Street, New York, NY 10017
www.businessexpertpress.com

ISBN-13: 978-1-63157-371-2 (paperback)
ISBN-13: 978-1-63157-372-9 (e-book)

Business Expert Press Marketing Strategy Collection

Collection ISSN: 2150-9654 (print)
Collection ISSN: 2150-9662 (electronic)

Cover and interior design by Exeter Premedia Services Private Ltd., Chennai, India

First edition: 2016

10 9 8 7 6 5 4 3 2 1

Printed in the United States of America.

Abstract

Service has a unique ability to create experiences that build profitable relationships with customers. Based on a service-centered perspective, this book analyzes the challenges of creating excellent customer experiences, including the management of technology and new media. It describes how customers coproduce and cocreate their experiences, and how these activities influence business revenues and costs.

Customer Experience refers to the sensory, cognitive, emotional, social, and behavioral dimensions of all activities that connect the customer and the organization *over time* across touchpoints and channels. It encompasses *all* activities involving the customer where the organization is the focal object, including prepurchase activities (such as exposure to a website ad), and purchase, consumption, and engagement behaviors (blogging, sharing photos). The book takes a deep dive into the psychology of customers, revealing the conceptual building blocks of customer experiences and how they build relationships over time. These ideas provide a business perspective on how customer-focused service strategies generate cash flows, including the role of pricing.

The book is designed to help managers translate customer insights into organizational actions by providing concepts and tools to:

- Uncover new sources of revenue from innovations and improvements in the customer experience, including leveraging business analytics and metrics (Chapter 6);
- Design service processes, operations, and channels to create customer experiences that build relationships, as well as design responses to service failures (Chapter 7); and
- Manage people and physical evidence in cocreating the customer experience, plus create a favorable service climate (Chapter 8).

The book closes by considering the customer experience from a global perspective and considering future business prospects.

Keywords

big data, business analytics, cocreation, customer equity, customer experience, customer journey, customer lifetime value, customer retention, design, digital media, innovation, loyalty, relationship, satisfaction, service

Contents

Acknowledgments

With gratitude and thanks to my colleagues and students.

CHAPTER 1

A Service-Centered View of the Customer Experience

Business in the 21st century is exciting: every aspect of the marketplace is being transformed. Technology is giving rise to new market opportunities, organizations are shaping and responding to markets in ways that are disruptive and challenging, and customer preferences and behavior are evolving rapidly. Organizations must focus on creating customer experiences that build relationships because they face new competitive pressures in a complex and dynamic marketplace. In this environment, many business experts have adopted a service-centered view because they believe that service, rather than goods, is fundamental to marketplace exchanges. This view has an inherent focus on the customer experience and the organization's entire relationship with the customer.[1] Services have traditionally been defined as deeds, performances, or actions.[2] However, today's managers often see their organizations as cocreating customer experiences that build relationships through service or solutions.

One definition of service is "applied knowledge for another party's benefit."[3] Based on this increasingly accepted definition, *all* aspects of product offerings (including goods, performances, and network exchanges) create service experiences that build relationships between organizations and their customers. Consequently, service organizations are diverse, including computing and information organizations (Cisco Systems), hotels and restaurants (Darden Restaurants), professional services (Accenture), banking and financial services (Charles Schwab), entertainment services (Disney), personal services (health, fitness, and recreation centers), Internet services (Google, eBay), and not-for-profit organizations (government services, museums and zoos, health, education, philanthropic, and public policy organizations). In addition, the service domain includes manufactured goods augmented with customer service—that is, service in support of an organization's core products, such as installation, billing, repair, and handling complaints. This book uses the word "product" to refer to *all* offerings—no matter where they fall on the continuum between (traditionally described) goods and services—because all offerings create service experiences that build relationships between organizations and their customers.

Research has shown that organizations with a strong market orientation are more successful.[4] A service-centered view is consistent with a strong market orientation because the organization focuses on creating customer experiences and building relationships by serving customers better than competitors. This book focuses on a service-centered view of the customer experience for three reasons.

1. Service has a unique ability to create customer experiences that generate bonds between organizations and their customers, as well as other key stakeholders (such as employees).
2. Service creates a differential advantage for an organization because customer experiences are difficult for competitors to imitate.
3. When markets change, a service-centered view places an emphasis on how organizations must learn and innovate so that their service strategies continue to create customer experiences that yield profitable relationships.

Case Study: Marriott Takes a Service-Centered View

Marriott International, Inc., operates and franchises hotels under 19 brands, with over 4,000 properties worldwide. Its brands include The Ritz-Carlton®, JW Marriott, Renaissance Hotels, and Gaylord Hotels. It was named one of the "World's Most Admired Companies" by *Fortune* in 2015. It regularly wins awards for customer service excellence and providing an outstanding workplace—a significant advantage in a highly competitive industry. It has continued to adapt and innovate in areas such as sustainability and managing diversity. In 2014, the company reported record revenue of $13.8 billion; net income was up 20 percent to $753 million, also a record.

Eighty percent of the U.S. economy is service-based. The economies of developed countries are primarily service-based and services are increasingly dominant in the global economy. Service industries include government, transportation, communications, finance, hospitality, education, retail trade, arts organizations, computing, and information services. IBM—originally a computer manufacturer—is now a service organization that emphasizes smart services, such as business process management and analytics. In addition, customer service augments or supports virtually all organizations' products (goods or services). Even organizations that produce so-called commodities must take orders, manufacture products that match detailed specifications, schedule deliveries, handle scrap materials, and process bills. For example, Alcoa Inc. is involved in mining, refining, smelting, fabricating, and recycling aluminum, titanium, and nickel. However, its expertise in providing business customers with products and solutions is responsible for making it one of the world's largest lightweight metal manufacturers in 2015. Hence, many thought leaders argue that every business is a service business.

Service is also important beyond the organization. It has a profound influence on the quality of life of people everywhere, as well as the societies they live in. By pursuing improvements and innovations in service, organizations are able to design and deliver services that increase people's well-being. Around the world, people are being lifted out of poverty by advances in health, education, and environmentally sustainable services. For example, for-profit and not-for-profit organizations seek to eliminate malaria. Major advances have been made in controlling malaria in developing nations in the past decade. Organizations have worked together to develop preventive health services, including timely diagnosis and treatment; patient education; spraying with safe; long-lasting insecticides; and distributing bed nets to protect people from mosquito bites. Service is transforming people's lives for the better everywhere. Through service, organizations—both for-profit and not-for-profit—are helping people achieve their aspirations for personal and societal well-being.

This book takes the perspective that excellent service creates customer experiences that build relationships. It will:

- analyze the challenges of creating excellent customer experiences, including the role of technology and new media (Chapter 2);
- identify how customers participate in their services experiences, including coproduction and cocreation—and their effects on how organizations manage demand and supply (Chapter 3);
- describe the psychology of customers, how they respond to service experiences, and how customer experiences can build relationships over time (Chapter 4);
- provide a financial and business perspective on how to manage relationships with customers that generate cash flows and profitability, including the role of pricing (Chapter 5);
- suggest concepts and tools to uncover new sources of revenue from innovations and improvements to the customer experience, including the use of business analytics and metrics (Chapter 6);
- describe ways to design and manage service processes, operations, and channels to create customer experiences that build relationships, as well as how to respond to service failures (Chapter 7);
- analyze the role of people and physical evidence in creating the customer experience, as well as the need for a service culture and climate within organizations (Chapter 8); and
- consider the customer experience from a global perspective, as well as how service will create customer experiences in the future (Chapter 9).

This chapter begins by describing how excellent service creates customer experiences that build profitable relationships for the organization. In addition, it identifies some of the key challenges to creating excellent customer experiences.

The Customer Experience

What is "the customer experience"? This book uses the term to refer to the sensory, cognitive, emotional, social, and behavioral dimensions of all activities that connect the customer and the organization *over time*, including all touch points and channels (i.e., business-to-business [B2B], business-to-consumer [B2C], and consumer-to-consumer [C2C] interactions). This definition encompasses *all* activities involving the customer where the organization is the focal object, including prepurchase activities (such as exposure to an ad, browsing a website), purchase behaviors, consumption behaviors, engagement behaviors (blogging, sharing photos), and other nonpurchase activities. Figure 1.1 depicts the scope of the customer experience, which includes all the elements radiating out from the offering.

- At the center of the drawing is the organization's service offering as it is perceived by the customer—that is, the deed,

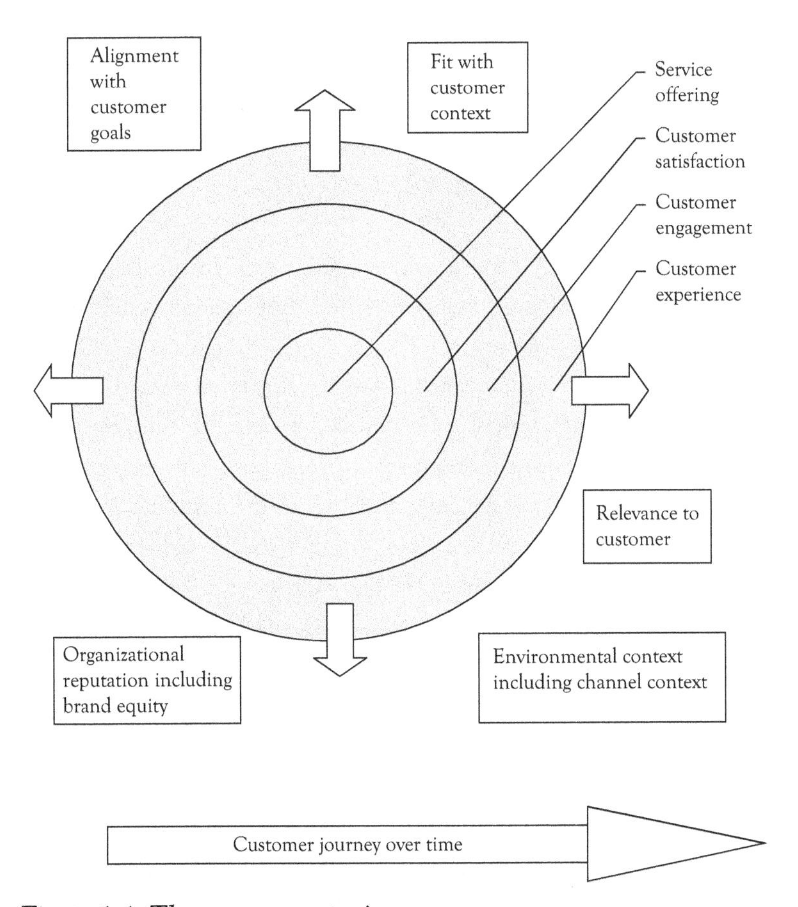

Figure 1.1 The customer experience

performance, or knowledge applied for the benefit of the customer. (The service may be cocreated with the customer.)
- The second ring depicts customer satisfaction—that is, the customer's purchase and postconsumption response to the service. Her satisfaction is formed after making multiple comparisons with expectations, emotional responses, judgments of fairness, and so forth.[5]
- The customer's engagement behaviors (i.e., nonpurchase behaviors) are depicted in the next ring; they include social responses for which the organization (or its offering) is the focal object, such as word-of-mouth interactions.
- The outer ring represents the customer experience. It encompasses all the aforementioned activities as they occur within a customer and environmental context that changes over time. Hence, the customer experience interacts with the organization's reputation, the alignment of its offering with customer goals, the fit of the offering with her situation or context, and the relevance of the offering to her.

Notably, Figure 1.1 shows the customer experience embedded in her unique situation (e.g., her goals), the organization's activities, and the broader marketplace context. A key feature of Figure 1.1 is that the customer experience encompasses a much broader set of activities and responses than organizations have usually considered. The inner circle depicts the customer-organization interaction that takes place when the offering is purchased and consumed. However, the customer experience goes beyond the customer's perceptions of the service and her satisfaction with the offering. As depicted in the outer circles, it is influenced by her engagement with the brand, which includes many nonpurchase activities (e.g., C2C activities where the brand is the target). The fourth circle shows how the customer experience encompasses all these activities—and also interfaces with her situation or context *at a particular moment in time.*

Figure 1.1 also emphasizes that all these activities are embedded in a specific context (characterized by goals, channel features, etc.) that magnifies or diminishes the effect of each experiential attribute.[6] Chapter 4 discusses how the customer takes a future-oriented perspective on how the customer experience contributes to her relationship with the organization. Lastly, her experience takes place over time—as it unfolds, the customer undertakes a journey with the organization.

The customer is the source of the organization's cash flows, so organizations must create excellent customer experiences to build strong relationships with them. Thus, business success is founded on cocreation: the organization cocreates experiences with customers over time that build the customer's relationship with the organization—and the relationship creates cash flows over time for the organization.[7] The customer experience is the linchpin of these cocreation activities. The relationship between the customer experience, the strength of the organization–customer relationship, and cash flows to the organization over time is depicted in Figure 1.2.

A service-centered approach to the customer experience builds relationships that lead to business success for two reasons.

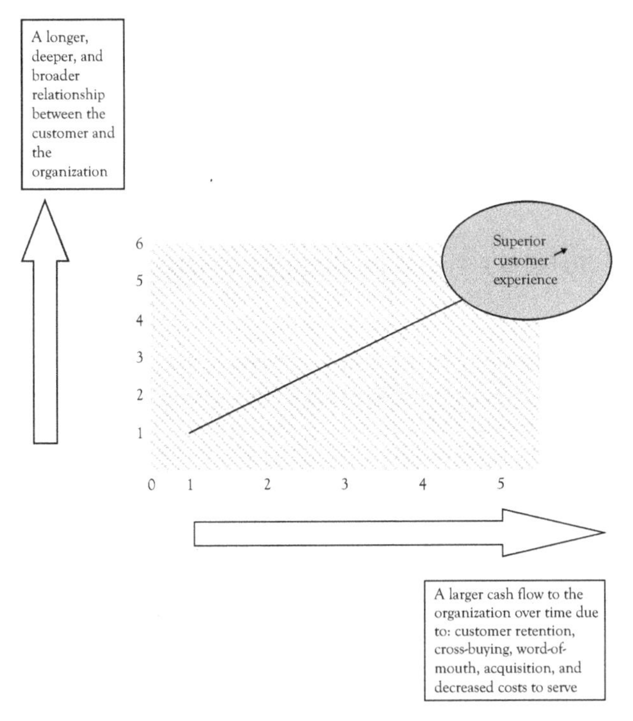

Figure 1.2 The effect of the customer experience on the organization—customer relationship

- By providing service that creates an excellent customer experience, organizations build strong relationships that increase customers' willingness to pay, loyalty and switching costs—ultimately leading to increases in firm profitability.[8]
- In strong relationships where both parties know each other well, service creates a competitive advantage by ensuring that their resources are used effectively and efficiently.[9]

Case Study: WeChat

WeChat is a mobile text and voice messaging communication service developed in China, first released in January 2011. Beyond messaging, it offers many benefits. Users can transfer money, purchase group discounts for activities, pay for taxis, book restaurants (similar to Yelp), book flights and train tickets, and so forth. It is very convenient, so that users' costs of switching to a competing service provider are high. For example, there are several ways to find friends and it can exchange contacts with people nearby via Bluetooth. The customer experience using WeChat's services is so favorable that its customers are extremely loyal, use its services heavily, and promote it to others.

Customer Relationships as Sources of Value

How do customer experiences build relationships that create cash flows for the organization? Some business experts distinguish three behavioral dimensions of customer–organization relationships that are sources of value:[10]

- Length or duration of the relationship
- Depth (amount or frequency of product usage)
- Breadth or number of different products purchased

Many studies have tracked individual customers and analyzed their experiences with service organizations over time in diverse industries, including telecommunications, entertainment, and financial services.

They show that an individual customer who has a high-quality service experience will have a longer, deeper, and broader relationship with the service organization than a customer who has a low quality experience.[11] These same linkages have been shown to exist at the firm level and across firms. Organizations have high market shares when customers have high-quality service experiences.[12]

Customers in a long-term relationship are more likely to pay a price premium and buy high margin products.[13] To compare their performance with competitors, organizations frequently track "share of wallet" or "share of customer"—that is, the amount of a customer's spending allocated to the organization expressed as a percentage of all the customer's spending in the category. When customers have longer relationships, organizations have decreased costs of serving them,[14] and a higher share of wallet.[15]

Organizations that deliver excellent customer experiences build longer relationships characterized by higher margins. Many cross-sectional studies show that organizations that deliver high-quality service experiences are more profitable.[16] Some firms, such as Sears, have implemented systems that collect and analyze customer responses to service efforts and then link them to consumer behaviors and financial indicators.[17] In summary, service strategies that deliver excellent customer experiences create relationships that are profitable for the organization.

Creating Profitable Relationships

Customer lifetime value (CLV) is a well-established measure of the value of an organization's relationship with a specific customer. CLV is a measure of all the future cash flows from the customer over the lifetime of the relationship less the organization's costs of serving the customer.[18] This metric has been in use for about 20 years; an early study calculated CLV in the newspaper publishing industry.[19] The CLV calculation can be performed for an individual customer, a market segment, or the entire customer base. Naturally, an organization cannot perfectly predict the cash flows associated with an individual customer, but it can calculate the expected value of the cash flows (adjusting for risk) associated with an individual customer conditional on the customer's characteristics, the organization's planned actions, and environmental factors.

CLV calculations can produce astonishing insights about the value of the organization's relationships with its customers. For example, the lifetime value of a customer who regularly visits a coffee shop can be thousands of dollars.[20] A telecommunications company estimated that a 10 percent increase in customer ratings from a better service experience was associated with an 8 percent increase in the duration of the average customer-company relationship and (consequently) an 8 percent increase in revenues.[21] CLV calculations are especially useful in guiding organizations on how to allocate their funds more effectively. Both the coffee shop and the telecommunications company made additional investments to improve customers' experiences based on their CLV predictions under different scenarios.

How can organizations create, maintain, and enhance relationships with their most valuable customers? Quite simply, customers will desire a relationship with the organization when its service creates an excellent customer experience. Both the organization and the customer must desire the relationship if it is to endure. When a customer (or market segment) has a high CLV, the organization should design service strategies that deliver excellent customer experiences that enhance the relationship. When the customer has an excellent experience but a low CLV, the organization should develop service strategies to improve the CLV from the relationship (or reduce the resources it allocates to the service experience).

***Point to Ponder*:** Many managers have argued that the secret to business success is simple: "Find and keep the right customers." Thus, organizations must gather information about customers, determine the expected future value of different market segments, provide service to targeted customers that creates excellent customer experiences, and generate value from the customer relationships. Are these activities feasible for all organizations?

Challenges of Managing the Customer Experience

There are many challenges to delivering an excellent customer experience in the modern marketplace. Traditionally, there has been an emphasis on the challenges of managing services, which are much different than tangible (manufactured) goods. The most apparent difference is that goods are associated with transactional marketing—that is, an emphasis on a single purchase occasion—whereas services are associated with cocreated customer experiences and (ultimately) relationships. In particular, there are four unique characteristics of service experiences that pose challenges for managers:[22]

1. Intangibility of the customer experience
2. Heterogeneity in experiences across customers and over time
3. Production and consumption take place simultaneously within the customer experience
4. Perishability of the offering

In addition to these four classic challenges, there are two modern challenges:

5. Infusing technology within the customer experience
6. Managing how new media shape and reflect the customer experience

Moreover, the organization must develop a coordinated approach to managing these challenges.

Table 1.1 provides a summary of these six challenges, and associated opportunities to create customer experiences that build strong and profitable relationships. The remainder of this chapter describes the first four challenges and current approaches for addressing them. Chapter 2 provides an in-depth discussion of the last two challenges—technology and new media—due to their critical importance to today's managers.

Customer Experiences Are Primarily Intangible

Intangibility means that customer experiences can't be seen, felt, tasted, or touched in the same way that people interact with tangible goods. Typically, they can't be inventoried or patented. In addition, despite some tangible aspects (e.g., facilities), customers typically find it difficult to evaluate the objective quality of their service experience. Instead, they form perceptions of (subjective) service quality. In these circumstances, organizations find it difficult to induce consumers to try new services and their pricing can be complex. For example, professional services—health care,

Table 1.1 Customer experience challenges and opportunities

Challenges	Opportunities
Customer experiences are primarily intangible	Insights into the customer experience can provide a differential advantage (Chapter 4) Innovate and improve processes (Chapter 6) Leverage physical evidence (Chapter 8)
Heterogeneity in customer experiences	Manage customer participation (Chapter 3) Manage partners and people (Chapter 8)
Simultaneous production and consumption during the customer experience	Design effective processes (Chapter 7) Develop recovery strategies (Chapter 7) Incorporate the customer into the innovation process (Chapter 6) Plan for customer participation (Chapter 3) Manage the customer mix (Chapter 5)
Perishability of the customer experience	Managing demand and supply (Chapter 6) Service design and multichannel management (Chapter 7)
Infusion of technology into the customer experience	Consider five roles for technology, beyond productivity improvements (Chapter 2) Integrate technology into the servicescape (Chapter 8)
New media shape and reflect the customer experience	New ways to leverage media (Chapter 2) New ways to manage physical evidence (Chapter 8)

education, financial, energy management, consulting, and information services—are frequently difficult for customers (consumers or business customers) to understand and evaluate.

Since experiences are intangible, a high-quality service has different meanings for different people, so organizations can create a distinctive customer experience for each individual. However, after many years of study and debate, most managers and scholars have agreed on several crucial distinctions. First, the consumption of a service is a subjectively experienced *process*, as well as an outcome.[23] Second, a customer's perception of the quality of the service experience consists of (at least) five underlying dimensions:

1. Reliability: performing the promised service consistently and accurately
2. Responsiveness: providing prompt service

3. Assurance: knowledgeable employees who convey trust and confidence
4. Empathy: caring and individualized attention
5. Tangibles: physical facilities, equipment, and the appearance of personnel[24]

The specific nature and importance of these five dimensions will be different for different organizations and service industries, but thousands of studies show that they tend to appear in virtually all customer service experiences.

Since the customer experience is primarily intangible—the consumption of a process—organizations require new approaches to innovation and improvement strategies (see Chapter 6). New service ideas may be reflected in proprietary business processes, which are difficult for competitors to observe and (consequently) imitate, thereby obtaining a differential advantage in the marketplace. For example, many innovative services for business customers are being built around data-driven customer insights. Managers must develop appropriate strategies to protect these intangible services (which usually can't be patented), communicate quality (through service branding), and support complex price strategies (tiered pricing).

A service brand isn't just a symbol or marketing communications plan. A service brand is the centerpiece of a strategy that positions the organization versus its competitors and articulates the promise it makes to customers about the service experience.[25] The promise can be communicated in many ways (see Chapter 8). For example, Mayo Clinic sends many signals—through employee actions, facility design, and customer-centered nursing and office practices—that demonstrate its commitment to a high-quality health service experience in concrete ways.[26] Building a service brand requires cross-functional coordination of these activities. Companies as diverse as Wells-Fargo (banking) and FedEx (shipping and supply chain solutions) have developed powerful brands and communication strategies to signal the quality of their services. Symbols can be used to convey intangible dimensions of the customer experience, such as reliability. For example, consumers learn to associate "the rock" with The Prudential Insurance Company of America and a distinctive brown and gold shield with UPS. Chapter 8 discusses how to leverage tangible or sensory cues within the customer experience.

***Point to Ponder*:** Timing is important to the customer experience. The time orientation of a person or culture can be categorized as monochronic or polychronic. Monochronic approaches to time are linear, segmented, and sequential. They are common in the United States, Germany, Switzerland, and Scandinavia. Polychronic approaches to time involve simultaneous actions and the involvement of many people, so the time it takes to complete an interaction is elastic and over-rides any schedule. They are common in Mediterranean and Latin cultures including France, Italy, Greece, Mexico, and some Eastern and African cultures. What does this suggest about managing global services for business customers? For consumers?

Heterogeneity in Customer Experiences

Heterogeneity refers to the fact that services are experienced differently across customers and over time. Each employee who delivers the service can be different; each customer who participates is different; and (consequently) the customer experience is uniquely personalized and customized. For this reason, almost every organization has difficulty delivering a consistent, reliable customer experiences across usage occasions. Many useful tools for managing quality were developed for the factory floor (e.g., Juran and Godfrey's [1999] *Quality Handbook*) not customer experiences, so such tools aren't necessarily applicable. A primary reason is that customers don't show up on the factory floor when goods are being manufactured, but customers are an integral participant in experiences—introducing variability into the organization's processes—when services are produced and experienced. Another reason is that outliers—which are typically avoided on the factory floor—might (or might not) flag a superior and unique customer experience.[27]

To address the challenges of heterogeneity in service delivery processes and outcomes, organizations must excel at human resource management, including the selection, training, and motivation of service personnel. They must also leverage their people's efforts by providing appropriate technology and monitoring and managing business processes so that customers' experiences match their specific requirements. For example, Johnson and Johnson, a manufacturer of consumer health care products and medical devices, has joined with other organizations to pursue advances in biotechnology and pharmaceuticals. In 2014, it became the first large medical device maker to share clinical trial data and diagnostic tests with university researchers. It is also involved with many programs that encourage healthy lifestyles and support those people who care for the health of others (such as nurses). Chapters 3 and 8 discuss how technology, partners, and employees can be leveraged to deliver superior customer experiences.

Point to Ponder: How do organizations use service strategies to increase spontaneity in the customer experience that enhances the customer relationship, rather than eroding the customer experience by creating inconsistency?

Simultaneous Production and Consumption Within the Experience

A good, whether it be a box of laundry detergent or a motorcycle or a forklift truck, is produced prior to the customer's experience with purchase and consumption. In contrast, customers are typically present and participate in their service experiences. In some situations, the presence of other customers during the focal customer's service experience means that failures may be visible to other customers and create ripple effects on the organization's relationships with them. For example, consumers give directions to the stylist when they have their hair cut; the service experience can be influenced by other customers who are also present in the hair salon. B2B suppliers, such as Cisco Systems, IBM, or Hewlett-Packard, work closely with their customers in selling and delivering complex business solutions. The capabilities of the *customer team* will influence the ability of the supplier team to design and deliver an excellent service experience.

The presence and participation of the customer during the service experience has three important implications.

1. Organizations must develop—and implement—efficient and effective business processes that enhance the customer experience (see Chapter 6).
2. Organizations will frequently find it useful to decentralize operations through multiple channels so that service experience takes place at locations close to customers (see Chapter 7).
3. Organizations must be prepared for service failures (which will inevitably occur), and develop recovery strategies appropriate to the customer experience.

Certain companies, such as the Walt Disney Company and Chik-fil-A, are widely admired for designing processes that deliver excellent customer experiences, anticipating potential service failures and developing appropriate responses, thereby leading to successful business outcomes.

***Point to Ponder*:** Under what conditions will the organization consider it efficient, effective, and profitable for customers to participate in creating a service experience?

Perishability of the Customer Experience

Perishability means that the customer's service experience cannot be inventoried or stored, or resold or returned. Capacity is available at a certain point in time: a seat is open on an airplane, a consultant has a block of time on his or her schedule, a restaurant has a fixed number of cooks, tables and waiters, computer server has fixed capacity, or a logistics supplier has a fleet of trucks and planes ready to depart. Unfortunately, if the service isn't utilized, it can't be saved for another day or another customer. If demand for a service exceeds capacity, the organization will typically lose sales unless the customer is willing to wait.

Service organizations must find effective ways to manage capacity and thereby match the supply of services with customers' usage of them.

Price is an especially powerful tool, but easily misused. For example, transportation services (airlines, trains, and city transit companies) use peak load pricing and hospitality and recreational services (golf courses and resorts) use seasonal pricing and reservation systems to smooth demand. However, more complex strategies require effective marketing communications, as well as the management of service capacity. For example, the United States Postal Service utilizes advertising and promotional activities to ask customers to mail their letters and packages early during the holiday season—as well as hiring and training additional employees, renting additional facilities, and so on. In particular, good predictive models help the organization better match supply and demand, so that customers have better experiences (see Chapters 3 and 6).

Point to Ponder: Swisscom Mobile, a telecommunications company, has no interest in outsourcing its customer service because it sees service as a way to set it apart from the competition.[28] Although it has a large market share, its size makes it vulnerable to upstart companies. When does it make sense for organizations to outsource aspects of service operations to third party organizations such as PeopleSoft, a provider of human resource management systems?

Cross-Functional Coordination

These four challenges must be addressed through integration across traditional functional silos to achieve a consistently excellent service experiences that enhance relationships with customers. Seamless and consistent service requires coordination of marketing, sales, human resources, operations (including supply chain or logistics functions), and information technology. Executing a high level of integration and coordination across so many organizational activities is extremely difficult. Perhaps this heightened need for coordination explains why so many organizations have appointed a customer experience manager at a senior executive level.

The customer experience is a lens for examining every organizational activity—from design through to delivery of the experience. Indeed, executional excellence is a form of competitive advantage—an advantage that competitors find difficult to imitate. For this reason, many managers subscribe to a holistic view and view the organization as a service system that delivers service experiences for customers. Managers must consider service processes, people, and physical environment—as well as the traditional organizational functions: product, distribution, promotion, and price. Into this mix, they must also consider the challenges of incorporating technology and new media into all of the activities of the organization. The next chapter discusses these two challenges.

***Point to Ponder*:** How does cross-functional coordination lead to superior service and excellent customer experiences? (Hint: What happens when marketing is "too successful" and an organization generates demand that can't be met through current supply chain arrangements?)

Key Ideas

- A service-centered perspective of management is based upon a broad definition of service design and delivery as "applied knowledge for another party's benefit."
- Service has a unique ability to create customer experiences that generate bonds between organizations and their customers, as well as other key stakeholders (such as employees).
- Service creates a differential advantage for an organization because customer experiences are difficult for competitors to imitate.
- When markets change, a service-centered view places an emphasis on how organizations must learn and innovate so that their service strategies continue to create customer experiences that yield profitable relationships.
- The customer experience includes the sensory, cognitive, emotional, social, and behavioral dimensions of all activities that connect the customer and the organization *over time*, including all touchpoints and channels (i.e., B2B, B2C, and C2C interactions).

- The customer experience encompasses *all* activities involving the customer where the organization is the focal object, including prepurchase activities (such as exposure to an ad, browsing a website), purchase behaviors, consumption behaviors, engagement behaviors (blogging, sharing photos), and other nonpurchase activities. It takes place within a customer and environmental context that changes over time.
- There are six major challenges to managing the customer experience. Each also presents opportunities:
  - Customer experiences are primarily intangible which provides opportunities for differentiation.
  - Customer experiences are experienced differently across people and over time, so people, processes, and technology must be used to ensure consistent and customized experiences for each individual.
  - Production and consumption take place simultaneously within the customer experience, so organizations must plan for the presence and participation of customers.
  - The customer experience is perishable, so organizations must match supply and demand in a variety of ways.
  - Advances in technology provide many different opportunities for the infusion of technology.
  - New media are shaping and reflecting the customer experience.

Notes

1. Lusch, Vargo, and O'Brien (2007); Vargo and Lusch (2008); Lusch, Vargo, and O'Brien (2007).
2. Berry (1980).
3. Vargo and Lusch (2004, 11).
4. Narver and Slater (1990).
5. Oliver and Swan (1989).
6. Bolton et al. (2014).
7. Gupta and Lehmann (2005, 44).
8. Anderson and Sullivan (1993); Heskett and Schlesinger (1994) Loveman (1998).

9. Heshmati (2003).
10. Bolton, Lemon, and Verhoef (2004).
11. Bolton and Lemon (1999); Bolton, Lemon, and Verhoef (2008); Crosby and Stephens (1987); Verhoef, Franses, and Hoekstra (2002).
12. Danaher and Rust (1996); Kordupleski, Rust, and Zahorik (1993); Rust, Zahorik, and Keiningham (1995).
13. Bolton, Lemon, and Verhoef (2008); Kamakura et al. (2003); Kumar (1999); Verhoef, Franses, and Hoekstra (2002); Verhoef (2003).
14. Reinartz and Kumar (2002).
15. Heskett and Schlesinger (1994); Mende, Bolton, and Bitner (2013); Reichheld (1992); Reichheld and Teal (2001).
16. Anderson, Fornell, and Rust (1997); Reichheld and Sasser (1990).
17. Rucci, Kirn, and Quinn (1998); Heskett and Schlesinger (1994).
18. Berger and Nasr (1998).
19. Keane and Wang (1995).
20. Moon and Quelch (2003).
21. Bolton (1998).
22. Zeithaml, Parasuraman, and Berry (1985); Zeithaml and Bitner (2000).
23. Grőnroos (1988, 1990); Rust and Oliver (1993).
24. Parasuraman, Zeithaml, and Berry (1985a, 1988).
25. Bitner (1995).
26. Berry and Bendapudi (2003).
27. Bolton, Lemon, and Bramlett (2006).
28. Logue (2006).

CHAPTER 2

New Challenges: Technology and New Media

Organizations must pay special attention to the role of technology and new media in the customer experience. Today, technology-enabled services are pervasive in relationships between organizations and their customers. Consumers use online banking services, digital services (music), location-based services (parcel tracking), mobile services (car telematics), and "smart" services (home security). Businesses use digitally delivered services (system support), network services (file sharing services), and cloud services enabled by a shared pool of configurable computing resources. Moreover, interactive services are pervasive in both consumer and business interactions. "Interactive services" refers to services characterized by customer–organization interactions which are supported by *any* level of technology.[1] Moreover, technology has enabled new media, including digital and social media. New media afford many opportunities for organizations to engage with customers in unexpected ways. In addition, many new media (unlike traditional media) offer opportunities for targeted, customized, and personalized communications in business-to-business (B2B) and business-to-consumer (B2C) markets.

Infusion of Technology Within the Customer Experience

Advances in technology are changing the customer experience by enabling organizations and customers to interact in new ways during service design and delivery. Interactive services don't just take place online. For example, the Peninsula Shanghai is a luxury hotel that uses smart systems to deliver customized in-room services (environmental controls), as well as customized services delivered by highly trained staff who are supported by technology (concierge services). In the future, the "Internet of Things" (IoT)—that is, the network of objects embedded with electronics, software, sensors, and network connectivity—will enable new services for both consumers and businesses based on the ability of these objects to collect and exchange data. Some experts predict that the IoT will include 200 billion things by 2020, which should enable exciting new data-driven insights that lead to new services for customers. Wearable technology (e.g., the Apple Watch and Fitbit) will become more sophisticated (as machines talk to each other), and dramatically change people's lives. In its *Technology Vision 2015* report, Accenture identifies an emerging trend that it calls "Workforce Reimagined," in which more natural human interfaces, wearable devices, smart machines, cognitive assistants, and other intelligent technology "interact as a team member" working alongside employees.

A key question for many service organizations is how best to deploy technology to create better service experiences and achieve a competitive advantage. The initial reaction of many managers is to consider technology as a way to reduce costs and make other resources more productive. However, technology also provides opportunities for better coordination, service improvements, and innovations that enhance the customer experience and generate new sources of revenue. There are (at least) five major considerations for service organizations deciding how best to deploy technology.[2] Technology enables:

1. Customer self-service that substitutes for employee labor;
2. New forms of support that complement employee efforts;
3. Customized service that improves the customer experience;
4. Information sharing among organizations and customers to improve service experiences and outcomes; and
5. Opportunities for innovation that generate new revenue streams.

This chapter discusses how each of these options has different opportunities and challenges, and then turns to a discussion of new media.

***Point to Ponder*:** The IoT will create vast amounts of data. Some experts predict that, by 2025, 85 percent of things will be connected to the Internet. How will your organization manage these data? What are the coordination challenges?

Self-Service Technology Substitutes for Employee Efforts

Many organizations use technology to encourage customer self-service, thereby reducing labor costs. For example, supermarkets have adopted self-checkout machines because one employee can run four to six checkout lanes while the role of the cashier is carried out by the customer. In this scenario, self-service technology becomes a substitute for employee labor. However, service organizations shouldn't blindly adopt self-service technology as it can potentially lead to the dangerous mindset that customers are "partial employees." Notably, the customer's participation can influence the quality of the service experience. Hence, organizations must ensure that customers understand the roles they play during interactive service experiences.

Case Study: Kaiser Permanente Introduces Interactive Services

Kaiser Permanente has developed innovative health care services to improve patient well-being. Its integrated management of patient care emphasizes preventive health care services, such as smoking cessation and weight loss programs. Many member services are available through an online portal: patients can send e-mails to care providers, review laboratory test results, and so forth. In this way, Kaiser Permanente has been able to simultaneously improve the patient's experience and well-being, as well as reduce costs. After its launch in 2009, more than 50 percent of patients adopted use of its web portal; 58 percent of those enrolled in an online support program stopped smoking and 56 percent in another program lost weight. In essence, Kaiser Permanente has created a novel business model for health care with different sources and uses of cash flows. Health service providers in other countries, such as the United Kingdom, have been studying its model.

Kaiser Permanente's experience shows how organizations must be creative and flexible in how they use technology as part of the customer experience. At the same time, managers must recognize that not all customers are willing or able to use technology effectively. It is incumbent upon managers to think carefully about how they will introduce new technology and coach customers on how to use it (see Chapter 3).

Organizations can also generate data-driven insights about consumers by analyzing customer records that are naturally generated as part of service provision. For example, Amazon offers products and services on many platforms. By analyzing integrated customer records, it can identify opportunities for new products (goods or services), which provide a superior customer experience. This capability led Amazon to develop a new B2B service, called QuickSight. This product is very fast, cloud-powered business intelligence service that provides visualizations, performs ad-hoc analysis, and helps organizations generate business insights from their data; it also delivers business insights in response to queries by employees within the organization.

Technology Supports and Complements Employee Efforts

Technology can be considered a complement, as well as a substitute, for employee labor. Many organizations have invested heavily in information technology systems so that they can serve customers better. The support of technology, coupled with intensive training and coaching, can help employees perform tasks that deliver a better customer experience, as well as successful business outcomes. For example, Harrah's Entertainment obtained a leading position in the gaming industry by developing sophisticated models of customer behavior and translating them into guidelines for employees. Employees are given "real-time" guidance based on business analytics regarding how to serve individual guests, including when to offer complimentary privileges (e.g., beverages, meals, and expedited service), cash awards and special offers based on play. Harrah's service-centered perspective has led to financial success by creating a customer experience that results in loyal customers who are responsive to its service and marketing activities.

A key consideration is whether technology usage interrupts or enhances the flow of customer–employee "scripts" that guide how people behave during service experiences.[3] When technology plays a role in delivering the customer experience, rapport-building efforts by employees must be carefully calibrated to be synergistic with technology in creating a superior customer experience. Otherwise, technology can conflict with rapport-building—and vice versa—with detrimental effects on the customer experience. On the plus side, frontline technology can mitigate poor service delivery by frontline employees who (perhaps) lack rapport-building skills.

In a B2B context, Oracle Field Services recognizes that—to provide an excellent customer experience—their field employees must be very technically skilled. However, they will also require extensive support in the form of data (such as technical specifications, diagrams, and pictures) and solutions. This support will be stored in the Cloud (i.e., hosted services on the Internet), rather than dedicated servers. Oracle managers envision a future when field employees will choose the channel and device most suited for their task and information needs: phones, tablets, computers, and machine-generated diagnostics. To support employees, Oracle's field service software integrates data from a huge number of sources, including machine-generated data and customer service data. In this way, field employees can deliver a customized service experience to customers in diverse environments.

Point to Ponder: In what ways does your organization ensure an excellent service experience when it is delivered remotely? How does it motivate and enable customers to use self-service technology? How do these strategies and tactics align with your brand positioning? What are the trade-offs in terms of cost savings versus employee-delivered service?

Technology Customizes Service to Match Customer Needs

Technology can facilitate customer participation that improves the quality of the service experience, service usage, and purchase behaviors, and thereby increases organization efficiency, revenues, and profits. For example, the

Hermes Group specializes in supply chain management services and solutions throughout Europe. It became Germany's largest independent home delivery operator (i.e., parcel service) by adopting innovative practices that blend technology-enabled tools (for managing shipping and tracking) with employee-delivered customer service. Customers can drop off or pick up parcels at a nearby shop, as well as temporarily store parcels. In this way, Hermes uses technology and customer participation to customize its services to customer needs—making it more effective—as well as standardize its services—for example, making it more reliable and responsive. This example also illustrates how technology can provide customers with different options for service delivery (i.e., service channels), which give them a sense of control, thereby improving the service experience. Chapter 3 is devoted to discussing the ramifications of customer participation—because it has become so important in today's customer experience. Chapter 7 discusses the design and delivery of service through different channels.

Technology Facilitates Information Sharing

Information technology provides many opportunities to learn and utilize information from customers, thereby creating a better experience. Some organizations have used data-driven insights to design new services for customers. Dupont Pioneer was able to leverage its biotechnology knowledge and expertise to identify new services that augment its sales of agricultural products (such as seed and fertilizers). For example, it helps farmers map and plan how best to replace nitrogen in their fields. Ultimately, Pioneer created a new service channel, Encirca^{SM} services, that provides customized insights and solutions regarding land management. This service channel opened up an entirely new market for the company. Chapter 3 discusses why information sharing is so crucial to the design and delivery of the customer experience—and to the organization's development of profitable customer relationships.

Data-driven customer insights are important to business success in today's marketplace. Customers often participate by sharing information about their needs and expectations, but some customers have privacy concerns about sharing personal information. Many highly publicized data breaches of retailers have heightened consumers' concerns about privacy.[4] People expect to be able to control how their personally identifiable information and other sensitive data—for example, health care records and financial records—are collected, stored, and analyzed. Their desire for control extends to e-mail, photos on social networking sites, personnel records, and so forth. Privacy issues frequently arise when organizations use improper or nonexistent information controls and safeguards for customer data. For this reason, it is vitally important for organizations to stay abreast of information disclosure guidelines set out by industry and government bodies—and to follow security procedures scrupulously, such as encrypting sensitive data.

Technology Provides Opportunities for Innovation and Growth

Advances in technology provide opportunities for organizations to innovate—in small ways and large. Technology can create new channels, help coordinate functions or channels to better serve customers, and generate new revenues. It can also provide benefits to customers, such as time and cost savings, convenience, and a sense of control. For example, Alibaba.com, a Chinese e-commerce company, was founded in 1999 to take advantage of opportunities arising from the convergence of four technology trends: the rise of the Internet, the global revolution in retailing, the prevalence of mobile phones, and the abundance of small and medium size manufacturing companies in China. Today, it is spectacularly successful in bringing together buyers and sellers through its web portals. It also offers a shopping search engine and cloud computing services. Importantly, its electronic payment services provide a trustworthy platform for buyer–seller relationships in a society with low trust levels. Innovation and improvement of the customer experience is a high priority for all organizations. Hence, Chapter 6 focuses on ways for organizations to identify new market opportunities, as well as innovate and improve the customer experience.

***Point to Ponder*:** Technology has fueled a "data explosion" in many organizations. How can your organization deliver an excellent customer experience with these data? How can your organization serve new markets with these data? Ask yourself: "Which potential customers would see our data as valuable?" "How can insights from our data be used to provide solutions to new customers?"

The remainder of this chapter discusses a pressing challenge that has arisen from advances in technology: the proliferation of new media.

New Media Shape and Reflect the Customer

New media afford many opportunities for organizations to engage with customers in unexpected ways. In addition, many new media (unlike traditional media) offer opportunities for targeted, customized, and personalized communications with B2B and B2C customers. In contrast with mass media, two-way conversations between organizations and their customers are possible. Digital media are forms of digitized content (i.e., text, audio, video or graphics) that can be transmitted over computer networks or the Internet. For example, organizations use digital media when they utilize websites, online ads, television advertising, mobile platforms, and so on. Social media can be defined (broadly) as any online service through which users—consumers or business customers—can create and share content. They include user-generated services (such as Snapchat, Twitter, or blogs), social networking sites, online review or rating sites, virtual game worlds, photo and video sharing sites (Instagram, Vine), and online communities through which consumers produce, design, publish, or edit content. Businesses are also becoming very active in cyberspace—both anticipating and responding to customers in new ways.

Most people consume (rather than contribute to) online media—obtaining information, enjoying leisure or entertainment, socializing and experiencing a sense of community, and staying in touch with friends.[5] Social media may clash with an organizations' branding and messaging, making it more complex to manage service brand images and customer experiences.[6] A particularly vivid example is Dave Carroll's YouTube video, entitled "United Breaks Guitars," which became an Internet sensation in 2009—creating a public relations disaster for United Airlines. There are many websites that offer online product reviews (such as Yelp Corporation, Amazon.com, Inc., and TripAdvisor, Inc.), thereby amplifying customers' word-of-mouth. Although organizations can't control social media, they can track, analyze, and respond to online communications. In addition, social media provide many opportunities to interact with customers, enhancing customers' experience with the service brand, thereby improving business outcomes.[7] Thus, organizations must find ways to harmonize their activities across all media and channels—both traditional and new—as well as contend with competitor and customer activities.

What are some of the ways that service organizations can use digital and social media to enhance the customer experience and obtain a competitive advantage? Social media experts argue that "Done right, social media strategies put the brand to work for customers."[8] They argue that managers should begin by thinking about customers' goals in using social media; this starting point ensures that service brand communications are integrated and aligned with customer needs and online behavior. Research suggests that people have four major goals in using new media:[9] **C**onsume (content), **C**reate (content), **C**onnect (with others), and **C**ontrol (privacy and information access), where goals may be combined (such as consume and connect). For example, American Express launched "Small Business Saturday" in 2010. The campaign went viral and encouraged consumers to shop with local merchants. This campaign aligned the goals of shoppers and merchants with the goals of American Express. It also helped people connect and access unique content about local product offerings.

In the remainder of this chapter, we discuss how new media can provide:

1. Sources of market intelligence to improve the customer experience
2. Avenues for building brand or user communities where customers share experiences
3. Tools to foster customer engagement
4. Channels to deliver customer service
5. Approaches to managing employees

Sources of Market Intelligence

Social media can be a source of market intelligence. Many organizations monitor social networking sites and blogs to collect relevant information pertaining their offerings (such as Twitter and Facebook) or purchase reports from market research suppliers (such as Shopzilla or Nielsen BuzzMetrics). In this way, organizations can learn about how customers feel about their service experiences, the nature and extent of customer word-of-mouth communications about the service brand, and how the brand's communication efforts are viewed. It is especially useful to track social media over time or combine with traditional media (because the two multiply each other's effectiveness). Many managers especially value the capability to stay abreast of changes in the marketplace. However, although social media are a timely source of market intelligence, it is important to recognize that people who post online are not necessarily representative of the entire customer base and their postings are sometimes driven by social dynamics (such as the need to stand out, impress others, or conform to prevailing opinion), which come from outside the realm of their customer experience.

Ideally, the firm's goal is to use this information in real time to design and deliver better customer experiences. More generally, consultants and analysts are harvesting data from platforms, such as Twitter or Facebook, with the goal of improving service by better targeting of customers. Large organizations, such as Amazon and eBay, use business analytics to develop customer insights from the massive amounts of data that are generated by their service operations. Sometimes, it is possible to develop predictive models so that the organization can anticipate customer needs. For example, IBM acquired The Weather Company because predictive models of the weather can help its business customers anticipate and plan for their customers' needs for different products and services. This new capability allows IBM to help its business customers better manage their supply chain—creating entirely new value-added services. Chapter 6 discusses the uses of business analytics and metrics further.

Avenues for Building Brand or User Communities

Organizations can create customer experiences and strengthen relationships by encouraging customers to engage with the brand and by fostering online brand or user communities. Brand or user communities are a web of relationships between the customer and the brand, between the customer and the firm, between the customer and the product in use, and among fellow customers.[10] Organizations can strengthen brand communities by facilitating shared customer experiences so that the service experience is embedded in a rich and dynamic social context. Quintessential examples of consumer brand community activities are

"Jeep Jamborees," family oriented, four-wheel-drive, off-road adventures, and Harley Owners Group® events for members which include cross-country trips. These lifestyle communities create unique social and emotional bonds between the organization and the customer.

The same social and emotional bonds can be formed by brand communities in the online world. In 2015, Starbucks Coffee was the second largest brand on Twitter in the United State, and it also has a significant presence on Instagram. Zynga is a provider of social video games. It is probably best known for Farmville, which was launched in 2009. Online communities also exist for B2B organizations, such as IBM Business Analytics User Groups and SAP User Groups. In user groups, people are able to share their knowledge, experiences, and ideas. These activities deliver an engaging customer experience with the service brand that strengthens the relationship between the organization and its customers.

There are many studies showing that social networks influence new product adoption.[11] However, studies of how social networks influence customer retention are much more limited. Notably, a recent study showed that the influence of social network on customer defection is as much as (if not higher than) its influence on adoption.[12] For some companies, customer referrals on social network sites seem to have more powerful and long-lasting effects than traditional media.[13] Moreover, one recent study found that—after joining an online community—customers increased their online purchases by 37 percent and their offline purchases by 9 percent.[14] Therefore, communities or social networks can increase the organization's cash flows, as well as enhance the customer experience and strengthen customers' relationships with the organization.

Tools to Foster Customer Engagement

Customer engagement behaviors are embedded within interactive, cocreative experiences with other parties involved in specific service relationships. They have the potential to create emotional and social bonds between customers and the target brand or organization, thereby creating a competitive advantage. For example, IKEA® and LEGO® have passionate fans who enjoy coming up with new ways to use their products—not all of which are company approved (for health or safety reasons).

Organizations can reap benefits from customer engagement behaviors—that is, word-of-mouth activity, photo or video sharing, blogging, and other nonpurchase behaviors that arise from motivational drivers with a brand or organization target.[15] For example, Pinterest is a forum for sharing images; the focus is on pictures, not text. However, clicking on an image will take you to the original source, so, for example, if you click on a picture of an item of clothing, you might be taken to a site where you can purchase it. Consumers use Pinterest to share their passion for fashion, art, architecture, and so forth.

Organic (i.e., customer-initiated) engagement behaviors are likely to be more effective in enhancing relationships with customers than engagement behaviors initiated by the organization—but both can be effective. Firm-initiated engagement activities can be effective if they align with customers' goals and emotional needs. Consequently, organizations launch holiday campaigns, sponsor sports teams, and initiate viral campaigns to build relationships. In a B2C context, these activities range from the "Ice Bucket Challenge" that raised money for the ALS[16] Foundation to Nike's "just do it" campaign. Both campaigns connected with customers on a large scale. The organization can create a shared history with the customer through engagement behaviors. For example, the American Express Company, a provider of financial services, has been an official sponsor of the U.S. Open since 1994. In addition to supporting the sport of tennis, the organization is able to offer unique experiences to members at tennis events, which deepen its emotional and social bonds with customers.

B2B organizations use service to create bonds with customers through.[17]

- Financial programs, such as discounts or economic incentives;
- Social programs including shared meals and entertainment; and
- Structural programs that increase the buying firm's productivity and efficiency.

Structural programs are especially effective due to the increasing availability of data generated by hardware and software, coupled with business analytics. For example, sales teams at companies such as Cisco Systems and Oracle deliver enhanced customer experiences through data-driven services and strengthen relationships, thereby creating a competitive advantage in the fast-changing business landscape.

Channels to Deliver Customer Service

Organizations can leverage digital and social media to deliver service and enhance customer experiences. For example, Jet Blue Airways has created a team that monitors and responds to customers via social media. They are trained and supported to act as customer service agents—for example, rebooking flights for passengers stranded by severe weather. Many Jet Blue customers find it easier and faster to simply tweet when they encounter a difficulty during their travels. In the same way, some restaurants offer "tweet-ahead" seating. From the customer's standpoint, new service channels offer convenience, cost and time savings, better access (e.g., 24 hour service), and emotional rewards. Many organizations have embraced the use of new media as a cost-effective way to deliver benefits that improve the customer experience. For example, with the emergence of the IoT, consumers might buy a refrigerator that can recognize when milk runs low and send an online order.

Shopping now takes place through numerous channels: in-store, online, by catalog, and within mobile phone applications. New media are transforming customers' retail service experiences in dramatic ways. For example, The North Face, an outdoor apparel and equipment retailer, has partnered with Jaunt (a technology company), to create an immersive, virtual reality experience (www.jauntvr.com/tnfrelease/). At selected North Face stores, consumers will be able to put on a headset and become immersed in an exciting outdoor experience, at locations such as Yosemite National Park, alongside well-known outdoor athletes. In this way, The North Face creates bonds—emotionally and socially—with shoppers, sharing their passion for outdoor adventure. These experiences also show outdoor apparel and equipment being used in compelling ways that are likely to stimulate purchase and usage. Chapter 7 discusses the challenges of service design and channel management in more detail.

New Approaches to Managing Employees

The increasing use of social media has important ramifications for how organizations hire and manage employees. These implications are especially significant in service industries, such as hospitality, where increasing numbers of Generation Y and Z (Gen Y and Z) members are entering the workforce. Gen Y and Z members were born after 1981. They are sometimes called the "Me Generation." They are digital natives who grew up in the Internet age and are savvy using technology to obtain content and connect with others.[18] Social media offer new opportunities for hiring, training, and supporting Gen Y and Z employees.[19] Chapter 8 discusses these opportunities further. However, organizations must be very cautious about using personal information from social media for human resource decisions due to employees' concerns about information sharing and privacy—potentially harming morale and productivity. There may also be legal constraints that vary by country.

***Point to Ponder*:** Some firms have used new media to embrace cause-related marketing and communicate to consumers and employees that they are striving to be socially responsible—and to foster emotional and social bonds. What might be the "dark side" to these efforts?

Key Ideas

- Technology infusion can change the customer experience through:
  - Customer self-service that substitutes for employee labor;
  - New forms of support that complement employee efforts;
  - Customized service that enhances the customer experience;
  - Information sharing among organizations and customers that improves service creation and delivery, yielding better outcomes for customers; and
  - Opportunities for service innovation.
- New media shape and reflect the customer experience. They can provide:

- o Sources of market intelligence to improve the customer experience;
- o Avenues for building brand or user communities where customers share experiences;
- o Tools to foster customer engagement;
- o Channels to deliver customer service and experiences; and
- o Novel ways of managing employees.

- There is no "one-size-fits-all strategy" for infusing technology and new media into the customer experience. Each offers specific opportunities and poses specific challenges.
- Customers' and employees' utilization of specific technologies and new media will depend on their goals, capabilities, and acceptance of each.
- The organization's capability to coordinate across functions and activities is crucial.

Notes

1. Bolton and Saxena-Iyer (2009).
2. Bitner, Brown, and Meuter (2000); Meuter et al. (2000, 2005).
3. Giebelhausen et al. (2014).
4. Hardekopf (2015).
5. There are generational differences in how people interact with digital and social media. See: Bolton et al. (2013) for an in-depth treatment of Gen Y and Social Media.
6. Bolton et al. (2013).
7. Lovett, Peres, and Shachar (2013).
8. Hoffman and Fodor (2010, 48).
9. Hoffman and Novak (2012).
10. McAlexander, Schouten, and Koenig (2002).
11. Peres, Muller, and Mahajan (2010).
12. Nitzan and Libai (2011).
13. Trusov, Bucklin, and Pauwels (2009).
14. Manchanda, Packard, and Pattabhiramaiah (2012).
15. Van Doorn et al. (2010, 254).

16. ALS is the acronym for Amyotrophic Lateral Sclerosis (often referred to as Lou Gehrig's Disease). See www.alsa.org/fight-als/ice-bucket-challenge.html?
17. Berry (1983); Palmatier et al. (2007).
18. Bolton et al. (2013).
19. Solnet and Hood (2008, 2010).

CHAPTER 3

Customer Participation and Its Implications for Managing Demand and Supply

Our discussion of the challenges of designing and delivering an excellent customer experience has emphasized that customers are present during the service experience *and* that their participation can have favorable or unfavorable effects on the customer experience. This observation is connected to a key tenet of a service-centered view, namely that that customers and organizations cocreate experiences. Although customers have always participated in service, rapid advances in technology and media have offered new ways for organizations to cocreate, engage, and build relationships with customers.

Customer participation is evident in both consumer and business markets. A.G. Lafley, chief executive at the Procter & Gamble Company (P&G) once remarked, "Consumers are beginning in a very real sense to own our brands and participate in their creation."[1] For example, P&G provides a Crest Whitestrips® website where consumers can watch a video demonstration about using the product, as well as learn how to follow a comprehensive dental system that matches their dental needs (www. whitestrips.com). In business-to-business (B2B) markets, Shell Brazil combines customized analytic capabilities with its portfolio of lubricants to work with customers to improve their machine performance. Construction equipment manufacturers ship unassembled parts to new geographic markets and then assemble equipment tailored to local business requirements.[2]

This chapter explores the implications of customer participation for the organization. It begins with the question: How should organizations manage customers' participation in the service experience? Managers may find it useful to distinguish between two types of participation:

- Coproduction: participation within organization-defined parameters
- Cocreation: participation with spontaneous, discretionary behaviors

Each has different implications for managing the customer experience. Then, this chapter turns to challenges of matching supply to demand when customers participate in the creation of their experiences.

Coproduction Experiences

Coproduction occurs when customers participate in service design and delivery *within organization-defined parameters,* thereby influencing customers' perceptions of the quality of the service experience.[3] In coproduction, the organization shapes how participation takes place. Usually, tasks are transferred from the organization to the customer, such as when business customers use FedEx software to begin the shipping process.[4] A services-as-theater metaphor suggests that customers are participants who need to know the "script" that will guide their roles or performances.[5] Hence, organizations must prepare customers to perform their roles, using employees and marketing communications, to ensure excellent customer experiences. Moreover, service experiences take place in physical surroundings, called servicescapes, which influence both customers and employees.[6] For example, a meal in a quick-service restaurant requires that customers follow a mutually understood script that guides how they place an order, fill a beverage cup, take their food to a table or select it from a buffet, obtain condiments and clear their table (see Chapter 8).

Coproduction takes place when the customer is present during service production and delivery, or when his or her possessions are present. When the customer is present, service processes, the servicescape and employee actions are highly visible and heavily influence the quality of the customer experience. Even when the customer participates by telephone or through computer-mediated channels, the service experience can still be very powerful—such as in shopping and gaming environments. (Customers can be seeking fun and adventure during their service experience.) When the customer's possessions are physically present but the customer is not—for example, an item is dropped off for repair—the service outcome (rather than the process) may be the primary influence on the customer's perceptions of the service experience.

Case Study: The Rise in the Sharing Economy

The rise of the "sharing economy" has sparked intense interest in services generated through online platforms that allow people to coproduce in new ways (e.g., Blablacar, Etsy, Funding circle). For example, Airbnb is an online marketplace facilitating short-term rentals ranging from a shared room or apartment to an entire house. Uber provides a smartphone app that enables ride-sharing using personal vehicles. Similar to Alipay, the platform acts as a mediator so trusting relationships can be formed. Although people have always shared and collaborated, these new online service providers make coproduction easier by bringing together buyers and sellers. Interestingly, these services seem to *increase* the potential market for accommodation and transportation services—as well as sometimes acting as substitutes for existing services (such as hotels and taxis or rental cars). Since these services are relatively novel, governments in some countries are grappling with how best to regulate them.

Cocreation Experiences

Cocreation occurs when the customer participates with the organization through *spontaneous, discretionary behaviors* to uniquely customize the service experience (beyond the selection of options predetermined by the organization). For example, consumers cocreate the experience of participating in a NASCAR event and Proctor & Gamble colocates its personnel at Wal-Mart to cocreate supply chain synergies. In both cases, the companies create customer experiences that cannot be created when the organization works independently.

The essential activities for cocreation are two-way communication between the customer and the organization, sharing of information and an explicit sharing of risk. Cocreation is pervasive for health care, education, financial, entertainment, and recreation services. For example, weight loss clinics, such as Jenny Craig, require compliance from customers—as well as discretionary effort (e.g., meal planning) to be effective in delivering their service.[7] In B2B experiences, cocreation occurs when service suppliers work closely with lead users, communities of users or engage in one-to-one solution selling. For example, the Annual Teradata PARTNER User Group Conference and Exposition brings together thousands of companies who share solutions relevant to data warehousing.

Both business-to-consumer (B2C) and B2B customer participation includes information sharing—that is, codified and tacit knowledge exchange.[8] Codified knowledge refers to knowledge that is transmittable in formal, systematic language whereas tacit knowledge is knowledge that is difficult to state explicitly about how to perform the function. Both types of knowledge are required for customers and service suppliers to work together. In particular, when each party shares their goals, expectations, and capabilities, organizations are better able to cocreate an excellent customer experience. This form of cocreation is especially apparent in B2B experiences, such as solution selling of high technology services, where services are designed and delivered over a period of many years. However, consumers also cocreate their service experiences, such as for professional services such as income tax preparation. C.K. Prahalad[9] pointed out that customer communities can shape the development of product strategy (for videogames) or new distribution channels (Napster). In this sense, he argues that goods and services are the "artifacts around which personalized experiences are cocreated."

High levels of discretionary effort by customers should reduce the costs of service delivery, as well as yield more customized and satisfying service experiences. However, there are two potentially negative consequences.[10]

- Customers who aren't competent in their service roles will have low-quality service experiences.

- A self-serving bias may operate such that customers who are heavily involved in cocreation may attribute successful experiences to their own efforts, and unsuccessful outcomes to the organization.

In complex B2B service experiences, such as consulting or other knowledge-based services (McKinsey, Nielsen), both parties share information about issues and problems, proactively working on the development and implementation of solutions. As services become more complex, both customers and employees require a clear understanding of their roles so that their role performance will be maximally effective in coproducing a high quality experience. Otherwise, buyer–seller relationships are likely to be characterized by uncertainty and conflict. For example, a manager recently held a special meeting to identify the root cause of certain customer experience problems. He brought together supplier and customer teams in a room where tables and chairs were in a circle to emphasize an egalitarian, sharing environment and to forestall conflict.

***Point to Ponder*:** How do your customers participate in service design? In service delivery? Are there ways they could be better coproducers? How would the customer experience improve? How would results for your organization improve?

Managing Customer Participation

The proliferation of media and channels has increased the number of touch points between organizations and customers, so managers must think creatively about ways to design and deliver customer experiences. Customer participation can take place along a continuum anchored by high contact (a maximal role) or a low contact (a minimal role). For example, consumers may order theater or sports event tickets online (low contact), but consume them in a complex servicescape where service personnel are highly visible (high contact). Or, a consumer may purchase supplies at Home Depot and then complete a home renovation project after an in-store tutorial (i.e., a high participation) or she may purchase supplies and installation services (i.e., a low participation).

Customers' willingness to participate in coproduction or cocreation will depend on at least four factors.[11] Customers' decision to participate will be influenced by their:

- Motivations and goals;
- The emotional gratification of participating in the service experience;
- Their need to control their service experience; and
- Their perceptions of the trustworthiness of the organization.

As customer participation increases, perceived risk—that is, some of the uncertainty associated negative consequences of the experience—may shift from the organization to the customer. Perceived risk might include uncertainty about the firm's performance, financial, opportunity or time, safety, social, and psychological loss.[12] For this reason, customers were initially slow to adopt some new self-service technologies, such as automatic teller machines (ATMs) introduced by banks in the 1960s, but have readily embraced others, such as buying computers or books from Internet retailers.[13] The same phenomenon can be observed for cocreated services, such as theme park experiences.

Changing customer behavior isn't easy. The customer must perceive benefits to the change. However, organizations can influence participation levels in four ways, by:

- Clarifying customer roles;
- Reducing customers' perceptions of the different risks of participation;
- Improving the design of the physical environment; and
- Rewarding desired behaviors.

For example, airline companies encouraged consumers to use self-service machines to print boarding passes by temporarily providing personnel to demonstrate the equipment and reassure consumers regarding the new procedures, as well as providing incentives for compliance with the new procedures (reduced waiting time). Their efforts were very successful in overcoming customer reluctance to insert a credit card into the machine—raising concerns about privacy and potential financial risk. In the same way, theme park employees—costumed as different characters—interact with guests and encourage them to participate in playful activities. Investments in teaching consumers new roles will frequently pay off in the long run when organizations become more efficient and effective in creating service experiences that build relationships, plus releasing employees to serve customers in new ways.

Serving Different Market Segments

Coproduction or cocreation by customers can pose a significant challenge to managing the service experience. Different market segments (i.e., groups of customers) may desire different experiences, and organizations must design and deliver different offerings that meet their needs. In this way, customer participation will sometimes bring different groups together—where they might potentially conflict. Although they share the same service setting, organizations may offer a completely different service experience to each group—often by segregating customers in some way.

Case Study: The Hospitality Industry

The hospitality industry provides different customer experiences to different market segments. For example, both business and leisure travelers are served in the same airports, on the same airplanes, and in the same hotels—but often in very different ways. At the airport, many countries offer a registered traveler program, such as the U.S.'s Global Access program. For a fee, travelers can register and then enjoy expedited service through airport security and passport control. On the airplane, some travelers enjoy extra amenities in the first-class or business-class cabin that are not available to travelers in coach. (Not surprisingly, there is usually a curtain between cabins so that these distinctions are not easily visible.) In hotels, business travelers may need business office services whereas leisure travelers may need facilities and services for children. In an effort to segregate these two groups and deliver better experiences, hotels have designed concierge floors and recreation areas for adults and children (such as fitness rooms and game rooms). At some hotels, conference facilities are situated at some distance from areas, such as reception, where the two groups mingle. These customized services are embedded in the customer experience these organizations offer to each market segment—and service offerings are priced accordingly.

Interestingly, the same consumer may be a business traveler on one occasion and a leisure traveler on another. Hence, the market segments are situationally specific and the organizations must find ways to recognize each group and customize their service to deliver an appropriate experience. Since customers are cocreators, they frequently identify themselves to organizations (by registering for Global Access, enrolling in hotel member reward programs, by booking accommodations through conferences). These same principles apply to serving business customers. Often small business customers have different capabilities than large business customers, so they require a different customer experience.

Providing Guidance and Latitude to Employees

When the organization's service personnel work with customers to cocreate service, a critical managerial issue is the extent to which organizational processes give latitude or discretion to service personnel. For example, Starbucks' baristas are encouraged to interact with customers to cocreate the coffee experience—but timely service is also important. In highly complex services, service personnel exercise considerable judgment. For example, legal services, health care, architectural design, and other knowledge intensive industries require considerable judgment from service personnel. Thus, organizations must select, train, and support their employees so that they can be maximally effective in cocreating the customer experience.

Increasingly, customers and organizations interact through a variety of forums, so cocreation is more prevalent than managers realize. Retailers such as Nordstrom or Rainforest Café are generally considered to be service organizations, rather than sellers of goods, because they design and deliver a shopping experience that includes customized services that are cocreated with customers (such as personal shoppers or a gift registry) and a unique product assortment targeted at a specific clientele. Employees can play an important role in creating entertaining and enjoyable service experiences. For example, at Build-A-Bear Workshop, Inc. stores, interactive bear-making stations help children (or adults) create their very own personalized stuffed animal with hundreds of outfits and accessories. In B2B markets, the cocreation experience might take place over several years, such as when Lockheed Martin Aeronautics sells customized military aircraft to the government of the United States. In this situation, the customer journey is complex and dynamic. Customer and supplier teams work together to negotiate goals, needs, and expectations over time.

***Point to Ponder*:** Cocreation can put organizations and their customers in conflict. What are some examples from your own experiences?

Managing Demand and Supply for Services

The participation of customers during service experiences raises yet another challenge. Organizations may have difficulty matching supply to demand because customer experiences are produced and consumed simultaneously and they are perishable. For this reason, airlines, hotels, and other service organizations practice yield management (variable pricing depending on forecasts of future demand) to ensure that empty airline seats and hotel rooms are used. Marketers will find it useful to think about fulfillment challenges by asking two questions:[14]

1. How Constrained is Supply?
2. What is the Extent of Demand Fluctuations over Time?

First, supply is constrained when organizations invest in considerable physical infrastructure that sets an upper bound on customer service usage. For example, there are a fixed number of service bays in an automobile servicing shop and a maximum capacity for a natural gas pipeline. When demand exceeds peak capacity, customers may be turned away or have a low quality service experience (e.g., due to waiting, crowding, high utilization rates). Sometimes the supply constraints can be relaxed—for example, a restaurant adds tables on a patio or a logistics company rents additional trucks or outsources some activities.

Case Study: Alibaba Prepares for "Singles' Day" in China

E-commerce was 7 percent of GDP in China in 2013 which posed supply chain challenges during peak periods. Singles' Day on November 11 (11/11) has set worldwide records for electronic shopping. Alibaba, China's biggest online shopping company, processed more than $5.75 billion dollars in its online payments system.[15] In order to prepare, Alibaba added extra servers and enhanced logistics. It also allowed customers to begin putting items in their shopping carts before sales had actually begun. In these ways, Alibaba was able to offer a better customer experience.

Second, managers must think about how demand fluctuates over time. Is it predictable (seasonal or growing) or random? Are fluctuations in demand due to stable consumer preferences (such as holiday patterns) or can they be influenced by marketing activities? Are there ways to create a reservations system or yield management systems to ration demand? For example, the airline industry is subject to predictable seasonal variation in consumers' needs for transportation (such as during American Thanksgiving, August in Europe, or China's Spring Holiday). Airlines utilize marketing communications, pricing schedules and yield management systems to encourage people to fly at off-peak times and enjoy a better customer experience. These issues are discussed further in Chapter 5 ("Monetizing the Customer Experience") and Chapter 8 ("Physical Evidence," including Branding and Communications).

***Point to Ponder*:** Does your organization cross-train employees to handle peak demand periods? Are there ways for it to use part-time employees, outsource activities, or "stretch" facilities by working over-capacity? How does this affect the customer experience? What methods does your organization use to predict demand? To manage demand?

Responding to Demand Through Different Service Channels

The customer is usually present during service production and delivery in one of three situations: the customer goes to the service organization (such as entertainment and retail services), the customer and the organization communicate remotely (telephone, Internet, or e-mail), or the organization goes to the customer (such as landscape and housekeeping services). An organization may also have multiple sites to serve customers. Service delivery channels influence the organization's effectiveness and efficiency in designing and delivering the service—and consequently customer's perceptions of the service experience.

New channels may open up new markets and sometimes cause disruptions within industries. Alibaba Group has built rural service centers in hundreds of Chinese villages so that people can search for products online and place orders (as well as sell products) through its online marketplaces, Taobao.com and Tmall.com.[16] Employees help customers without Internet access and those who do not know how to shop or place an online order. With an economic slowdown in China in 2015, the rural service centers are an important opportunity for new growth for Alibaba.[17] Another e-commerce giant, Amazon, opened its first bricks and mortar bookstore in Seattle in 2015. The store is reported to be rather small, stocking about 5,000 titles, so observers are waiting to see how Amazon plans to use its new channel for growth and profitability.

For these reasons, it is useful for managers to consider what functions are performed during service experiences and whether they can be separated. Customer provision of information and payment can often be separated from service production and delivery. The telephone and Internet have led to the separation and proliferation of service delivery channels that support some or all such activities that were previously bundled. For example, Skype, Spotify, and Birchbox have disrupted traditional service channels for long-distance communications, music, and beauty services, respectively. A key driver of whether these services succeed or fail is the extent to which they provide convenience to customers. Manager can analyze the likely success of unbundling by considering five dimensions of service convenience: decision, access, transaction, benefit, and postbenefit convenience.[18]

Point to Ponder: What are some creative ways that other organizations match supply and demand during peak periods?

Multiple service channels raise challenges. For example, when does it make sense to deliver service to consumers through multiple channels? Is it possible to reach new markets? Managers must consider whether multiple channels provide consumers with opportunities to search more effectively, bundle services, reduce risk, and increase convenience. They cannot simply consider whether certain channels are more cost efficient. For example, customers' perceptions of risk—and their anxiety about whether the company can be trusted—influence their preferences for how they interact with financial services organizations, such as whether they would prefer a face-to-face visit or not.[19] Chapter 7 considers these issues in more depth in its discussion of multichannel management.

Point to Ponder: Charles Schwab & Company, a discount brokerage service, has multiple service channels, such as face-to-face, telephone, and computer mediated. Do they make it easier or more difficult to match services to customer needs? Why?

A Service Demand Typology

Service organizations may find it useful to classify services so they can generate insights about how to match market opportunities with organization capabilities. Many different classification schemes have been suggested. This chapter's discussion focuses on two enduring categories proposed by Lovelock.[20] It starts by asking two questions about the nature of the relationship between the organization and the customer:

1. Is the relationship continuous or discrete?
2. Is it a membership relationship?

In each situation, there will be a customer journey, but the journey will be quite different. The answers to these questions can be surprising. For example, Harley-Davidson Motorcycles discovered that its typical customer journey began with a store visit as a child, accompanying an adult rider; the average customer purchased a motorcycle much later in life.

Continuous Relationships Versus Discrete Transactions

In continuous relationships, service is delivered on an ongoing or intermittent basis. Consumer service experiences include telecommunications, financial, health, and public or government services, such as transportation. B2B service experiences include computing, maintenance, and logistics services. In discrete relationships, service is transactional. B2C examples include restaurants, movie theaters, and car-rental services. B2B examples include retail services, such as repair or printing services. Note that, even when services are discrete, customers may return, so there can be a sequence of service experiences. Continuous and transactional services are two ends of a continuum; customer experiences may fall in between. When service is transactional, it may be difficult for the organization to know whether it still has a relationship with a particular customer or if she has defected to a competitor.

Organizations are increasingly interested in creating customer experiences that build and enhance long-term relationships with their customers.[21] One reason is that organizations that are customer relationship-oriented seem to achieve higher returns on their investments over the long run than do transaction-oriented organizations in B2B experiences.[22] There are many ways that organizations can encourage consumers to move from transactions to relationships. Notably, organizations with better knowledge of their customers can provide better service experiences. For example, a B2B service supplier can build a customized online ordering system to strengthen its relationship with key customers. There are advantages for both parties: the customer typically receives customized service that improves his or her experience and the organization can price (more profitably) based on service usage.

Point to Ponder: In the 1980s, Taco Bell instituted a lean service process called K-minus.[23] The preparation of beef, cheese, and beans was outsourced to centralized commissaries so that each outlet could "shrink the average size of a restaurant kitchen by 40 percent, freeing up more space—and more employees—to serve customers." During the same time period, Dell radically changed the computing industry for similar reasons. It outsourced goods production to focus on service to customers. For each company, consider the nature of the customer–firm relationship (i.e., continuous or discrete), the nature of the service (i.e., person or possession), coproduction activities, and the role of the customer. Are they the same or different? What do these companies experiences suggest about coproduction that's relevant to your organization today?

Membership Relationships and Loyalty Programs

Many organizations that supply continuously provided services—such as medical, telecommunication, and financial services—naturally accumulate customer information over time which allows them to better serve customers. Often, service organizations create formal membership relationships so that the organization "knows" the identity of the customer—and, consequently, her preferences for service. Memberships enable organizations to more effectively and efficiently segment markets and deliver customized service experiences. For example, Costco Wholesale is a membership wholesale club that offers brand name merchandise and customized services. Other services that are able to leverage their membership records include arts organizations and fitness clubs. Memberships may be optional or required. For example, a consumer might buy a single theater ticket (no membership, just a discrete transaction) or buy a subscription (membership, relationship). Customers who appreciate a customized service experience are likely to become members—but some customers may still decline due to privacy concerns or for other reasons.

Sometimes service organizations launch loyalty programs to obtain some of the advantages of membership relationships—especially to learn more about customers and serve them better. For example, the Carlson Rezidor Hotel Group offers membership in a loyalty rewards program to its guests. Members provide information about the preferences and, in return, they have access to special benefits and privileges when they stay at any of its 1,000 hotels worldwide. These benefits are customized to match customer preferences for amenities, including early check-in, late check-out, and upgraded hotel rooms.

It is important to distinguish between loyalty programs that offer economic rewards from those that also offer social rewards.[24] Some loyalty programs primarily offer volume discounts—that is, "cash back" programs—so that they don't necessarily engender feelings of loyalty from customers. Instead, these programs create switching costs for customers, so that they are "locked in," at least for the short run. For example, an independent doughnut shop might give customers a card that is punched on every visit, with the tenth visit earning a free beverage or pastry. An astute shop owner might try to remember the customer's name and (perhaps) have his regular order ready, thereby creating social bonds that can lead to true feelings of attachment and loyalty. There is evidence that repurchase rates go up for customers participating in a loyalty program even after accounting for the effects of short-term promotions like e-mail coupons, pricing changes, or discounts in shipping fees.[25]

***Point to Ponder*:** Customer switching costs may include lost performance cost (e.g., loyalty rewards, volume based discounts), search costs (to find a new supplier), set-up costs, and sunk costs.[26] When customers share information with a service provider, what are some ways that organizations increase their customers' switching costs? What considerations encourage some customers to share their information?

Key Ideas

- Coproduction occurs when customers participate in service design and delivery within organization-defined parameters, thereby influencing customers' perceptions of the quality of the experience.
  - Organizations must ensure that customers are willing and able to participate and understand their roles, so that they can be effective in coproduction.
  - Organizations must provide latitude to front-line employees in how they carry out their roles, as well as guidance and support.
- Customers cocreate their experience by participating through spontaneous, discretionary behaviors, such as information sharing, so that their behavior may have a substantial influence on the quality of the customer experience.
  - As customer participation increases, some of the risks associated with the performance of the service may be shifted from the organization to the customer.
  - Customers' participation in the cocreation experience will depend on their motivations, the emotional gratification of participating in the service experience, their need to control their service experience, and their perceptions of the trustworthiness of the organization.
- Organizations are increasingly interested in creating customer experiences that build and enhance long-term relationships between with their customers to achieve higher returns on their investments.
- Organizations should consider diverse ways of managing demand and supply, rather than relying heavily on price.
- Loyalty programs offer an avenue to building relationships with customers—and help organizations learn more about customers to serve them better.
  - Social rewards foster customer engagement activities and further develop the relationship with the customer.

- o Economic rewards, such as volume discounts or "cash back" programs don't necessarily create an emotional response or strengthen the relationship.

Notes

1. Elliott Stuart (2006).
2. Booz-Allen Hamilton (2001).
3. Bendapudi and Leone (2003).
4. Chase (1978); Lovelock and Young (1979).
5. Grove and Fisk (1992).
6. Bitner (1992).
7. Dellande, Gilly, and Graham (2004).
8. Chesbrough and Spohrer (2006); Bolton and Saxena-Iyer (2009).
9. Prahalad (2004).
10. Bendapudi and Leone (2003).
11. Bolton and Saxena-Iyer (2009).
12. Cunningham (1967).
13. Meuter et al. (2000).
14. Lovelock (1992).
15. Wang and Pfanner (2013).
16. Roberts and Chen (2015).
17. *Businessweek* (2015).
18. Berry, Seiders, and Grewal (2002).
19. Mende, Bolton, and Bitner (2013).
20. Lovelock (1983).
21. Berry (1983, 25).
22. Kumar (1999).
23. Henkoff (1994).
24. Bolton, Kannan, and Bramlett (2000).
25. Lewis (2004).
26. Burnham, Frels, and Mahajan (2003); Jones, Mothersbaugh, and Beatty (2002).

CHAPTER 4

The Building Blocks of the Customer Experience

This chapter analyzes customer experience from the customer's viewpoint, rather than the organization's viewpoint. Subsequent chapters use this analysis to introduce some best practices for creating excellent customer experiences that build relationships. Recall from Figure 1.1 that the customer experience can be visualized in the form of concentric circles, beginning with the cocreation of the service, followed by her satisfaction and then her engagement; all embedded in a specific context characterized by her goals, the relevance of the organization's offering and other aspects of her situation or context. This chapter builds upon this conceptualization to develop a more in-depth understanding of the customer experience building blocks. This chapter does the following:

1. Introduces the moving staircase as a way of thinking about how the customer experience evolves over time, creating a customer journey.
2. Discusses how customer's motivations and goals provide a "frame" through which a customer views her entire experience.
3. Describes how she perceives the experience, where perceptions may not be the same as objective measures.
4. Explains how the customer evaluates her satisfaction by comparing her perceptions of the experience with different expectations or comparison standards, where she may use multiple standards from different sources.
5. Considers how customers rely on information cues to assess cause-effect sequences that take place during the experience.
6. Describes a customer's potential emotional responses to discrepancies between her experience and expectations.

7. Reviews different notions about fairness that customers may use in assessing their experiences.
8. Discusses the role of customer engagement activities within the customer experience.
9. Speculates about how customers look ahead to their next experience with the organization—considering factors outside their experience to date.

A Guide to the Customer Experience

This chapter uses a diagram to guide the discussion of the customer experience. Figure 4.1 shows a moving staircase composed of customer experience building blocks. The staircase is divided into steps based on the way that most organizations think about the customer experience. Specifically, most organizations make distinctions between service quality (at left), then customer satisfaction, customer engagement, and the customer experience (at right), where each concept is broader and more inclusive (The labels for each step are shown at the top of the figure.). Within each step, there are many building blocks or aspects of the customer experience.

There doesn't have to be any elapse of time between steps. The customer's experience takes place over time and, at any time, she will usually be able to form an assessment of each step. Hence, the customer experience is dynamic and iterative—almost as if the customer was on a continuously moving escalator where she can go up or down. However, from the organization's standpoint, the steps are very different. It is important to have a solid foundation before building the next step. For example, excellent service quality is a necessary (but not sufficient) condition to provide customer satisfaction—which ultimately leads to favorable engagement and a delightful customer experience. Hence, although the customer experience and journey are continuously changing over time, this chapter describes each step separately beginning with the first step of the staircase (on the left).

- *Step 1: Service quality*. The foundation of the customer experience is her perceptions of the quality of her experiences with the organization—in the context of her experiences with the competition and the marketplace. Recall that the customer

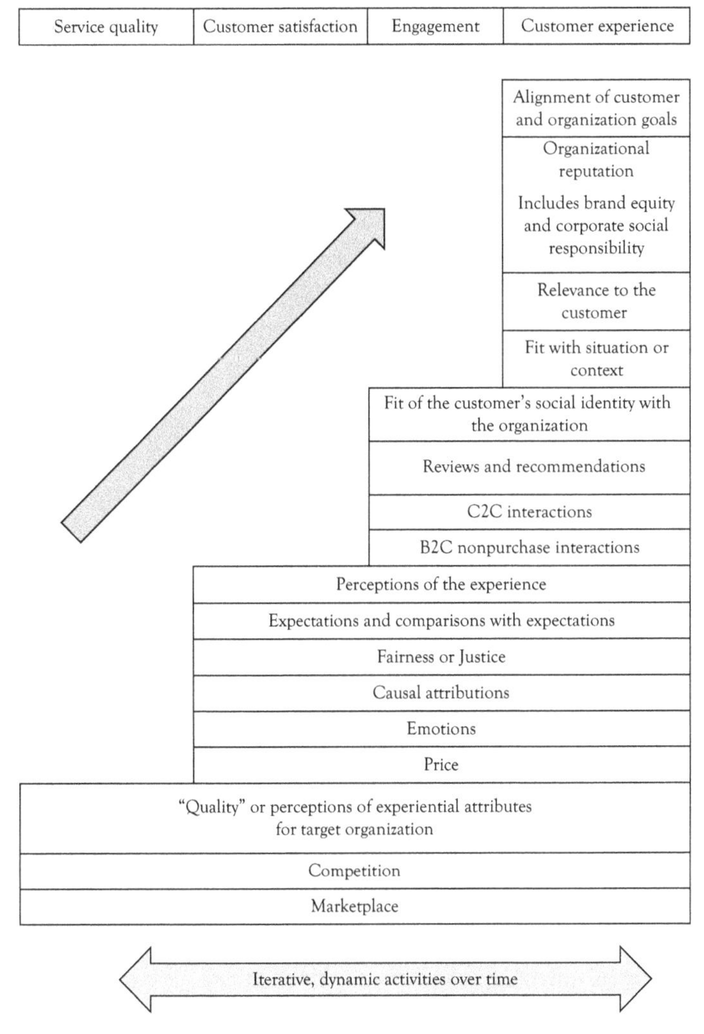

Figure 4.1 Customer experience building blocks: A moving staircase

participates and subjectively experiences both a process *and* an outcome.[1] Over time, she will experience multiple interactions entailing a process and outcome. At any point in time, she has a perception of *service quality*.

- *Step 2: Customer satisfaction*. On the next step of the staircase, the customer has an overall response to the purchase and consumption experience, termed *satisfaction*. This holistic response is influenced by perceptions, comparisons with expectations, emotional responses, and so on. These antecedents can be considered conceptual building blocks that organizations can use to create satisfying—and sometimes delightful—customer experiences.

- *Step 3: Engagement activities.* The customer is also (possibly at the same time) interacting with the organization in other ways (outside the purchase and consumption experience) as well as with other customers. Her nonpurchase interactions (such as visiting the organization's website, reading online reviews or interacting with other customers) are called customer *engagement.* Customer engagement can be considered in diverse ways. This chapter broadly considers four aspects of engagement: consuming reviews and recommendations, consumer-to-consumer (C2C) interactions, business-to-consumer (B2C), or consumer-to-business (C2B) nonpurchase interactions and assessments of the fit of the customer's social identity with the organization.
- *Step 4: Customer experience* (at a moment in time). The fourth step, on the right, shows the conceptual building blocks related to how the customer thinks about her experience and relationship with the organization *when looking to the future.* This step has also four conceptual building blocks, including the customer's goals and the organization's relevance to the customer in the future.

As the customer experience evolves over time, the customer journey is taking place. This journey will be a dynamic, cocreated process. It may not always be positive or favorable. Sometimes, a negative customer experience will cause the relationship to deteriorate.

The remainder of this chapter uses Figure 4.1 as a guide to discussing the building blocks of the customer experience.

Customer Motivations and Goals

The customer's motivations and goals are shown at the top of the staircase. They are discussed first because consumer's goals are very important in guiding their attention, perceptions, responses, and actions. People have practical and emotional motives (i.e., reasons) for engaging in relationships with organizations. Their motives influence their perceptions of the customer experience.[2] Practical motives include seeking products that solve a problem, efficient use of time and other resources, task-specific goals (e.g., price comparison), and collecting information.[3] People also have emotional motives. They are motivated to seek positive emotions and avoid negative emotions—even in computer-mediated channels that were once believed to be unconducive to emotions.[4] For example, the major reasons consumers give for an online or offline shopping trip are: adventure, gratification, to perform a role (e.g., parent shopping for back-to-school), value, social benefits, and idea generation.[5]

Often, consumers' motivations are related to their social identities. For example, a Phoenix Zoo visitor might be an outdoor enthusiast, an animal lover, an environmental activist, someone who enjoys social or community activities, or a parent enriching her child's life. Based on their motives, consumers will be driven to accomplish certain goals. For example, a shopper's motivation might be to express gratitude to a friend. Her motive will drive a specific goal, such as browsing to generate ideas. For shopping trips, most consumers report one of three goals: browsing, searching (which can include information acquisition, building knowledge, and deliberating), and buying. Social identities and goals frame how customers look at their experiences.

Consumers usually begin by choosing their goals and identifying ways to attain them. They can have multiple goals, where some are personal or situational, so it is important to understand the customer's context.[6] During the service experience, customers execute an action plan to achieve their goals, update their goals, and modify their action plan.[7] For example, a consumer might seek freedom and adventure. These emotional reasons lead to a specific goal, going on a trip on a motorcycle. Then, she enrolls in a motor riding class at Harley-Davidson Motorcycles, Inc. to get ready for the trip. People's motives and goals arise in both online and offline service channels.[8] Organizations can recognize customers underlying motivations and encourage them to make emotional connections to their service brands.

Case Study: Lowe's Connects with Customer's Motives and Emotions

Lowe's is a chain of home improvement stores that understands the ways that consumers' homes are part of their identity. The company connects with people through its emotionally resonant theme: "love where you live." The organization connects with consumers by telling stories about how people engage with the brand. In the store, it presents products through displays that allow the consumer to experience the product as she would at home. Professional customers (in construction and trade) represent approximately 30 percent of total sales; they desire a different kind of service experience that requires a knowledgeable service representative. In addition, Lowe's employees can connect with both consumers and professionals through their participation in the community improvement projects that it sponsors.

Managers must recognize that customers' goals magnify aspects of the service experience—so their perceptions may be quite different from "objective" attributes of the experience from an organizational perspective. For example, a consumer's goal in purchasing a prestige or luxury brand might be to wear it as a status symbol. By definition, status symbols aren't accessible to everyone, so exclusivity becomes an important aspect of the customer experience. When sales of luxury handbags grew rapidly in China, some brands opened many retail stores, thereby losing their aura of exclusivity. Their sales growth ultimately slowed. In contrast, luxury brands with small market shares, such as Miu Miu, were less likely to lose their aura of exclusivity. Their sales continued to grow.

This section has described how motivations and goals moderate (magnify or diminish) different aspects of the customer experience. Figure 1.1 shows that there are other contextual factors that can also act as moderators. Environmental or channel features also magnify different experiential attributes—even when the consumer has the same superordinate goal. For example, online customers may seek to minimize time and effort, which magnifies their perceptions of waiting times that are (objectively) brief. Hence, they may experience frustration when webpages load slowly or information isn't readily available—despite the fact that their wait times are faster than in-store waits. The discussion of other contextual factors is deferred until the end of the chapter. However, it is important to remember that they are all operating throughout the customer experience.

Service Quality

Now, let's take a deep dive into the customer experience—and analyze how it is cocreated by the customer and the organization. The discussion continues to use Figure 4.1 which shows the customer experience building blocks for the remainder of this chapter. It begins on the left with *Step 1* (*service quality*). Service quality is the foundation of the customer experience. Recall that the customer's perceptions of the quality of the service experience usually include five dimensions:

- Reliability or performing the promised service consistently and accurately
- Responsiveness or providing prompt service
- Assurance or knowledgeable employees who convey trust and confidence
- Empathy or caring and individualized attention
- Tangibles or physical facilities, equipment, and the appearance of personnel[9]

Many organizations survey customers and elicit ratings of the excellence or superiority of these five dimensions of the service experience. The survey items are often similar to the items in SERVQUAL, a highly influential and widely used questionnaire developed by services scholars.[10] For example, a sample item for a customer's perception of reliability might be: "When XYZ promises to do something by a certain time, it does so."[11] The respondent might be asked to rate the item on a 5- or 7-point scale anchored by agree and disagree. The nature of the survey items varies widely depending on the industry, the firm, the service channel, and so forth. For example, a survey designed for an online channel experience is quite different from a survey designed for an in-store experience.

Each organization must identify the experiential attributes that are important to customers in different contexts. Subjective perceptions of an experiential attribute (responsiveness) may be very different from organizational standards or performance measures of the same attribute (minutes elapsed). Hence, this information is central to understanding the customer service experience. However, customer perceptions are only the first step in understanding the customer experience. Next, the organization needs to understand the customer's *responses* to the cocreated experience: sensory, cognitive, emotional, and behavioral.

How Customers Assess Their Satisfaction with Consumption Experiences

Customer satisfaction (step 2) refers to the customer's responses to the purchase and consumption experience. People's response to experiences—especially consumption experiences—have been studied for many decades,[12] so business experts have a good understanding of how people evaluate their experiences. The conceptual building blocks of customer satisfaction are shown in the second column of Figure 4.1. They are:

- Perceptions of the experience
- Expectations and comparisons with expectations
- Fairness or Justice
- Causal attributions
- Emotions and
- Price.

Let's begin by considering overall satisfaction and its primary ingredient—perceptions of experiential attributes. Consumers are not cognitive machines. Their response to this comparison has an emotional component, as well as a cognitive component. They can be delighted with an exceptional service experience—or frustrated and angry when service is below par.

Customer satisfaction is the most widely used perceptual measure of experiences because it can be applied to almost any experience, including nonprofit and public services.[13] Even without a precise definition, customer satisfaction is clearly understood by consumers—and managers find it easy to communicate and interpret. It has been measured using many different scales; including better, same, or worse; very satisfied or dissatisfied; and poor or excellent. It also has a long track record; research findings are quite robust regardless of which scale is used. For these reasons, it is a very useful way to measure the customer's holistic response to a consumption experience.

Customers' satisfaction with the service experience is usually defined as a fulfillment response. It includes the cognitive and emotional responses to a consumption experience over a given time period. Customers' satisfaction depends on their perceptions of experiential attributes. Consumer's consider *all* aspects of their experience—even small details—and form a holistic evaluation.

Expectations and Comparisons with Expectations

Customers' perceptions of experiential attributes influence customer satisfaction directly, as well as indirectly via comparisons with expectations. This comparison process is so fundamental to the formation of customer satisfaction judgments that scholars call it "the expectancy-disconfirmation paradigm." The satisfaction formation process is quite straightforward. The consumer has expectations about a service. She compares these expectations with her perceptions of the experience. Her perceptions include sensory cues: sight, touch, hearing, smell, and taste. (We discuss perceptions further in Chapter 8.) If service is better than expected, the consumer is satisfied with the service experience. If service is worse than expected, she is dissatisfied. (These predictions ignore other factors that might operate.)

Case Study: First Direct Bank

A business blog featured a story about a woman traveling in London who discovered she had lost her purse.[14] When she began calling to cancel her bank cards, the customer service representative at First

Direct (a division of HSBC) offered to arrange for £200 to be collected from a bank near her hotel. All the woman had to do was tell the representative what she would be wearing when she went to the bank. This story illustrates how exceptional service exceeds expectations, generates an emotional response and favorable word-of-mouth. In this particular case, the woman's delight with her service experience led to substantial word-of-mouth effects as her story has been told (and retold) online and offline.

An added complication to understanding how consumers evaluate their service experiences is that they have more than one type of expectation. They frequently can't articulate the exact nature of their expectations prior to experiencing the service—but they recognize excellent service when they experience it.[15] There are (at least) three types of expectations that influence consumers' satisfaction:

- Predictive expectations ("What will happen?")
- Normative expectations ("What should happen?")
- Ideal expectations ("What is the best that can happen?")

Customers' satisfaction directly depends on their expectations, as well as indirectly via comparisons. For example, if a consumer expects poor service, she may decide not to repurchase from a retailer. Predictive expectations are usually based on past experiences or available information cues (e.g., marketing communications). Normative or should expectations are especially complex because they concern justice.

Consumers adjust their expectations based on their past experiences with a service organization or its competitors, marketing communications, price cues, word-of-mouth from other consumers, and other sources. In the First Direct case, it seems likely that the customer service representative exceeded all three types of expectations. Consumers may have very specific expectations about the different aspects of the service experience. For example, they usually want (and expect) service to be very reliable or consistent over time. When the service experience is better or worse than expectations, consumers are likely to look for the cause of the discrepancy.

For example, the woman in this story might attribute the cause of her excellent service experience to First Direct Bank's service culture and employee training—or to the particular customer service representative who handled her request. Her causal attribution may influence whether she expects the same level of service from First Direct in the future.

Consumers don't always articulate their expectations, but that doesn't mean they don't exist. For example, if asked "What do you look for in a refrigerator?" a consumer might reply, "I want an icemaker in the door." Yet, she will immediately notice if the refrigerator isn't keeping food cold—that is, her unstated expectation hasn't been met. Moreover, consumers may base their expectations on experiences in other product categories or service industries. In some cases, managers may feel that these expectations are unrealistic.

Fairness or Justice

Consumer judgments about fairness or justice are based on their normative expectations. They have (at least) three components.[16]

- Distributive justice ("What was my economic outcome?")
- Procedural justice ("What was the service procedure? e.g., first-come, first-served")
- Interactional justice ("How was I treated during the process?")

Organizations frequently focus on distributive justice, such as monetary compensation to a consumer for inconvenience, and overlook the importance of other aspects of justice. For example, "first come, first served" is an example of procedural justice and "providing a courteous explanation" is an example of interactional justice. In this way, even small details of procedures or interactions can become very important to consumers.

For example, if Amazon.com, Inc. can deliver an expensive designer handbag to a shopper within two days, why does she have to wait so much longer for a custom (bespoke) luxury handbag? Service organizations may need to pay special attention to communicating about the nature of the service—in this instance, the time and care that craftsman take in making a bag with unique features. With more knowledge and experience, consumers' expectations can become more context-specific.

Point to Ponder: Online shoppers browse when they have no immediate intention of making a purchase. Their behavior is emotionally driven and spontaneous. How can the organization distinguish them from shoppers who have a specific intention to compare offerings and make a purchase, so it can provide a better customer experience?

Causal Attributions or "The Blame Game"

When there is a discrepancy between expectations and perceptions, people usually seek a reason for it. People tend a "blame game" where they make causal attributions about whether a service outcome (success or failure) is due to the organization, an employee, a network partner (e.g., a supplier), or the customer. Customers frequently rely on extrinsic cues or signals observed in the servicescape to evaluate an experience. For example, they may assess whether the failure was preventable by the organization or due to circumstances beyond its control. Visible signs of adverse weather may suggest to an airline passenger that a delay in an airplane's departure is beyond the control of the airline—so she is *unlikely* to infer that the airline provided a poor experience. These causal attributions are another conceptual building block that influences satisfaction and (ultimately) the customer experience (as shown in column three).

Unfortunately, causal attributions don't always work in the organization's favor. A patient might infer from a messy or crowded waiting room that a doctor provides poor health care.[17] Or, an unpleasant odor in a grocery store might cause shoppers to evaluate a retail experience as poor—because the store seems to be paying insufficient attention to cleanliness. For this reason, the reliability or consistency of the customer's service experience is extremely important to service brands.[18] Marriott Corporation posts brand-specific service standards on its internal website, specifying "everything from cereal offerings at breakfast (oatmeal is required, grits are optional) to the way that napkins are folded."[19]

People generally prefer to have control over their service experiences, with the ability to make choices.[20] They can choose to control the environment or their own behavior (e.g., avoiding a crowded aisle in the store). The Internet of Things will enable organizations to offer customers more control over their service experiences through smart systems. For example, organizations already offer energy management systems that provide environmental control, entertainment systems that offer control over the service environment, and so forth. Managers will need to assess whether new connections among machines will make new cross-company or cross-industry collaborations possible. If so, they will need to seek out new partners and work with them to innovate in ways that build new and better customer experiences. These phenomena will make it more difficult for organizations to manage expectations and causal attributions, as well as the way experiences are cocreated.

***Point to Ponder*:** How is Amazon's website designed to be "sticky"—that is, so that consumers enjoy their shopping experience, stay longer, and buy more?

Emotions

Emotions are another conceptual building block that influences customer satisfaction and (consequently) the customer experience. Given their particular goals, customers will consider whether the service is better or worse than expected as described earlier. Then, depending on the discrepancy or gap between perceptions and expectations, customers will experience emotions such as anger, sadness, joy, and satisfaction.[21] Are there common human emotions that apply to all customer experiences? A good place to start is a checklist of 10 discrete emotions that scholars have used for almost 50 years.[22] They are:

- Interest;
- Enjoyment (fun, excitement);
- Surprise;
- Distress (sadness);
- Anger (frustration, annoyance);
- Disgust;

- Contempt;
- Fear;
- Shame or shyness; and
- Guilt.

Some studies have distinguished between positive and negative affect, where discrete emotions influence affective responses, such as like or dislike.[23] Emotions can have a very powerful effect on customer satisfaction and future behavior, such as magnifying the effects of experiential attributes. For example, when a consumer becomes frustrated with a long wait, she may pay even more attention to the waiting experience, such as counting the customers ahead of her in the line or checking her watch. In this way, her waiting experience becomes an influential determinant of her overall satisfaction.

Case Study: Multichannel Study by a Global Retailer

A global retailer recently analyzed over one million customer surveys across three channels: store, website, and catalog.[24] The retailer discovered that customers reported experiencing the same four distinct emotions when shopping in all three channels: enjoyment, annoyance, a sense of mastery (or control), and boredom. Shoppers reported enjoyment during the shopping experience, especially when they encountered new and inspiring ideas. However, managers were surprised when shoppers reported annoyance more frequently than expected. Further investigation showed that customers reported annoyance when their goal was to make a purchase (as opposed to browse) and they perceived that the website wasn't easy to use or the store wasn't easy to navigate. Managers concluded that the shoppers' goal-directed behavior (focused on an immediate purchase) was magnifying the effect of small details, such as waiting time experience, that were less important to shoppers who were spontaneously browsing. These findings led the company to consider ways to redesign both channels to be more flexible to better match the goals of customers focused on an immediate purchase—not just the customers who are browsing or searching.

Price

Perceptions of price and price fairness are conceptual building blocks of customer satisfaction and (ultimately) the customer experience. Price has a very powerful effect on customers, so managers must be very careful in their design and execution of pricing strategies. Consumer response to price is problematic because it influences consumers in four entirely different ways:

- Customers' prefer low prices to high prices, when all else is equal.
- Price can be a cue for quality.
- Price is used in judgments about fairness.
- Price judgments depend on context.

First, consumers generally prefer low prices when all else is equal. Their willingness to pay premium prices will depend on the benefits offered by the service. They often make judgments about what is a "low" versus a "high" price by comparing competing service offerings. Second, price can be a signal of quality. Consumers may use price as a quality cue when they lack any other information that might help them form expectations about the service experience. Consumers may actually prefer a high price (and presumably high quality) service over a low price (and presumably low quality) service. However, this situation is extremely unusual because there is almost always other information available in the market place. In particular, brand name is an important cue or signal that provides a great deal of information.

Third, price is used to make judgments about price fairness, thereby influencing consumer satisfaction with the service experience. Customer perceptions of price fairness depend on a variety of factors. At its most basic level, consumers make a comparison of what they are giving (price and nonmonetary costs) versus what they are getting (the experience). An important nonmonetary cost is service convenience (or rather its lack). Service convenience is the perceived time and effort associated with purchasing or using a service.

Fourth, consumers' evaluation of price fairness will also depend on context or situational factors. Their evaluations of price are likely to depend on their knowledge of prices and the extent of price variation in the marketplace.[25] Consumers are more likely to consider a price is fair when they know the underlying costs of designing and delivering the service.[26] For this reason, most people are willing to pay more for a soft drink purchased in a hotel bar than they are for a soft drink dispensed from a vending machine. Note that, in this example, value-added service allows the hotel bar to charge a price premium. Consumers also accept that there are price discounts for those who purchase in large volume or make early reservations, thereby helping organizations manage demand and supply. Consumers may also consider it fair that certain market segments, such as children or senior citizens, are eligible for lower prices. Similar factors operate for business-to-business (B2B) interactions, such as volume discounts or discounts for early payment.

Customer Engagement

The *customer experience (step 3)* encompasses more than satisfaction with the purchase and consumption experience. By explicitly including step 3, Figure 4.1 recognizes that the customer experience includes engagement behaviors—that is, social activities for which the brand is the target that take place over time. In the past, organizations couldn't always observe or track experiences such as B2C interactions with the brand (such as ad exposures) or C2C interactions about the brand. However, due to advances in technology and new media, organizations are now able to measure, monitor and—sometimes—respond to customer engagement behaviors. Consequently, as discussed in Chapter 2, organizations can leverage new media for their ability to reflect or shape customer behavior. An attractive feature of new media is that they provide timely information that opens up new ways for organizations to interact with customers. These opportunities will be described in more detail in Chapter 6.

Customer engagement encompasses a variety of social responses for which the brand is the target. (See Chapter 2's discussion of new media and social media.) The conceptual building blocks of customer engagement are shown in the third column of Figure 4.1. They include:

1. Generation and consumption of reviews and ratings;
2. C2C nonpurchase interactions (including word-of-mouth and observing other customers);
3. B2C or C2B nonpurchase interactions; and
4. Fit of the organizational identity with the customer's social identity.

First, customers may express purchase intentions or make recommendations on review sites or other forums. Their intentions are important because of the effect that they have on other customers, not because they are necessarily good predictors of future behavior. One reason why they may not be good predictors of future behavior is that circumstances will change. The customer's situation can change in the short run (e.g., she drives a different route to work and stops at a different store) or the long run (e.g., she moves to a new home). In addition, competitors change and the business environment changes. Reviews and ratings receive extra attention from managers because favorable word-of-mouth is important in building brand equity and the organization's reputation. A strong reputation makes customer acquisition easier and less costly. By advocating on behalf of your brand, customers are marketing your brand for your organization.

Second, there are many other ways that users can create and share content, including services such as Snapchat and Twitter, social networking sites (Facebook), online review sites (Yelp), virtual game worlds, photo and video sharing sites (Instagram, Vine), and online communities. Since these customer engagement behaviors (B2B, B2C or C2B, and C2C) are embedded within interactive, cocreative experiences with other parties, they have the potential to create emotional and social bonds between customers and the target brand or organization. For example, social media can be used to better serve customers (e.g., tweet-ahead restaurant seating) and respond to complaints. However, there are two important caveats.

- Customers' goals when they interact with each other (C2C) may be quite different than when they interact with the organization or a third party such as a review site. For example, customers may be motivated to help others or to advocate prosocial behaviors (e.g., sustainability) that are unrelated to their customer experience.

- Online activities are likely to reflect social identities of customers which may—or may not—be relevant and synergistic with the organization's brand.

The third building block of customer engagement is the fit or synergy between the organizational identity and the customer identity.[27] For example, suppose a customer's social identity as a mom is salient when she shares her parental experiences online. A diaper brand, such as Pampers® and Huggies®, might find an opportunity to affirm and support this identity, thereby improving her customer experience. In this way, the target brand increases the customer's identification with the organization. However, a similar intervention by another brand—not relevant to the customer's identity as a mom—would not have an effect on the customer.

A Future-Oriented View of the Customer Experience

All of the previous customer experience building blocks share an important disadvantage. *They are retrospective.* They look backward at the customer's experience with the organization, rather than forward.[28] In addition, most do not incorporate competition and cannot reflect or anticipate marketplace changes. Hence, managers should not expect that any single building block or measure can predict customers' likelihood of continuing the relationship with the organization. Instead, it is more helpful for organizations to use multiple perspectives or measures which, considered together, may provide a future-oriented view of the relationship between the service organization and its customers.

Thought leaders have proposed that the customer's evaluation of his or her experience with an organization should reflect the customer's hope for her relationship with the organization in the future.[29] In addition to the customer's goals (discussed at the beginning of the chapter), there are three building blocks that capture a context-specific and forward-looking perspective on the *customer experience (step 4).*

1. The organization has a trustworthy reputation.
2. The organization offers products (goods or services) that are relevant to the consumer.
3. The organization's products fit the customer's future situation or context.

Customers may consider a variety of factors in assessing the organization's reputation. Perceptions of corporate social responsibility play an important role in many customers' assessments of an organization's reputation.[30] Consumers may consider how organizational actions contribute to social welfare, including workforce diversity, sustainability, fair trade sourcing, and fair pay (e.g., in the food service industry). For many organizations, customer-based brand equity is an important component of their reputation (See Chapter 8.). Customer-based brand equity occurs when the consumer is "familiar with the brand and holds some favorable, strong and unique brand associations in memory."[31] For example, Coca-Cola has a favorable history and heritage for some consumers—reinforced by happy consumption experiences, such as family picnics. Some aspects of the organization's reputation will vary by industry. For example, some organizations are trusted to provide technological leadership (Google or Amazon) or safeguard people's health and well-being (government agencies, The Mayo Clinic).

The second conceptual building block, relevance, is a brand attribute that is tracked by media and market services suppliers. A recent academic study showed that two brand metrics, brand relevance and energy, provide incremental information (beyond accounting measures) in explaining stock returns, suggesting that it is a leading indicator for the trajectory of the customer-organization experience and relationship.[32] The underlying explanation is that customers' perceptions of brand relevance are early indicators of their willingness to continue in a relationship with the organization. For example, Starbucks customers consider the brand relevant to them, so they are willing to purchase products (such as music) at their stores, even when the products aren't closely connected to the Starbucks coffee experience.

Fit involves whether the organization has or will have something to sell that the other party wants to buy.[33] The notion of product-customer fit has been shown to explain customer's purchase behavior in many situations. However, it is especially helpful in understanding cross-buying behavior. For example, business customers will buy system support contracts that deliver high service levels (at high prices) to meet their need for maximum support of critical business processes.[34] Product-customer fit may depend on the social identity that is evoked in a particular situation. For example, a consumer may feel that purchases of Girl Scout cookies and Boy Scout popcorn are a good fit with her identity as a parent.

Reputation, relevance, and product-customer fit—along with the alignment of organizational goals with customer goals—are the forward-looking components of the customer experience. However, there is not (as yet) a great deal of information about how these conceptual building blocks influence the customer experience. However, many organizations measure and manage these building blocks, understanding that they contribute to business success through paths that aren't well understood. For example, many organizations pay attention to customers' perceptions of Corporate Social Responsibility; they consider actions that contribute to social welfare such as workforce diversity, sustainability, fair trade sourcing, and fair pay (e.g., in the food service industry). More generally, organizations must manage the "future promise" of the brand. For example, Amazon.com, Inc. began as an online bookseller and evolved into an electronic commerce and cloud computing company. Initially, its customers might not have imagined that they would eventually want (and buy) additional services from ranging from a digital media player (Fire tv) to cloud music services. However, loyal customers *trusted* Amazon, recognized that it offered *relevant* products and anticipated that it would offer new services that *fit* their needs.

Customer Journey

This concludes our discussion of the conceptual building blocks of the customer experience. In summary, the customer experience can be conceptualized as a moving staircase. Over time, the customer has interactions with the organization and other customers (about the organization). Most organizations make distinctions between customers' perceptions of service quality, satisfaction, engagement activities, and the customer experience. However, it is important to understand the conceptual building blocks that compose the customer experience and the mechanisms that link them. Again, the customer experience is dynamic and iterative. We call the customer experience over time the customer journey. The customer experience is constructed out of the conceptual building blocks, so it is constantly transforming over time. The customers' perceptions and behaviors change, as well. At any point in time, the organization can take only a snapshot of this moving target—or perhaps, try to predict where the customer is going in the relationship with the organization.

To create an excellent customer experience, the organization must begin with a solid foundation, service quality (step 1), cocreate purchase and consumption experiences that satisfy customers (step 2), engage with customers in ways that are mutually beneficial (step 3) and offer future experiences that fit customers goals and needs (step 4).

Thus, Figure 4.1 depicts conceptual building blocks that organizations must manage to create an excellent customer experience. Together, they form a reasonably comprehensive picture of the customer experience. To manage these building blocks, organizations must measure and track them—and take actions to influence them, thereby creating favorable experiences. Chapter 5 describes how organizations can derive cash flow streams by managing customer experiences and relationships over time. Then, Chapters 6 to 9 discuss managerial actions that can create customer experiences that build relationships.

Key Ideas

- Customer experience includes four building blocks:
    1. Customer perceptions of cocreated experiences before, during, and after purchase and consumption—including perceptions of product quality (including both goods and services).
    2. Satisfaction ingredients, such as the customer's perceptions of her experiences, comparisons with expectations, causal attributions, emotions, and judgments of fairness, including perceptions of price.
    3. Customer engagement activities, including in consumption of reviews and ratings (which influence brand equity), C2C and

B2C or C2B activities, and the fit of the customer's social identity with the organizational identity.

4. A "forward-looking" component that reflects the customer's hope or assessment of the future of the relationship with the firm. It includes an assessment of how well customer and organizational goals are aligned, the organization's reputation, the relevance of the organization to the customer, and the offering's fit with the customer's situation or context.

- Customers' motivations and goals guide their attention, perceptions, responses, and actions. Goals can be practical, such as seeking a product that solves a problem, or emotional, such as fun or adventure.
- Goals and emotions can magnify different aspects of the customer experience.
- The customer experience is dynamically constructed out of these building blocks, so it is constantly changing over time.
- The customer experience over time is called the customer journey. At any point in time, the organization can only take a snapshot of this moving target—to help predict how the customer–organization experience is changing over time.
- From the organizations viewpoint, it is necessary to build a strong staircase (as shown in Figure 4.1). Each step is a foundation for the next step.

Notes

1. Grőnroos (1984, 1988, 1990).
2. Babin, Darden, and Griffin (1994).
3. Noble, Griffith, and Weinberger (2005).
4. Wang, Minor, and Wei (2011).
5. Arnold and Reynolds (2012).
6. Ratneshwar et al. (2001).
7. Bagozzi and Dholakia (1999); Campbell and Warren (2015).
8. Wolfinbarger and Gilly (2001).
9. Parasuraman, Zeithaml, and Berry (1985a).
10. Parasuraman, Zeithaml, and Berry (1985a, 1988).

11. Parasuraman, Zeithaml, and Berry (1988).
12. This chapter draws heavily on research by Richard L. Oliver. An excellent resource is Oliver's (2015) book.
13. Zeithaml et al. (2006).
14. Bolton et al. (2014).
15. Oliver (2015).
16. Smith and Bolton (1999).
17. Bitner (1992).
18. Bolton, Lemon, and Bramlett (2006).
19. Jackson and Sanders (2006, 6).
20. Hui and Bateson (1991).
21. Nyer (1997).
22. Izard (1991); Richins (1997); Westbrook and Oliver (1991).
23. Oliver (1993).
24. Tarasi et al. (2015).
25. Zeithaml (1988).
26. Bolton and Alba (2006).
27. Fombelle et al. (2012).
28. Zeithaml et al. (2006).
29. Zeithaml et al. (2006).
30. Sen and Bhattacharya (2001).
31. Keller (1993).
32. Mizik and Jacobson (2008).
33. Fombelle et al. (2012).
34. Bolton and Myers (2003); Bolton, Lemon, and Verhoef (2008).

CHAPTER 5

Managing Customer Relationships to Achieve Growth and Profitability

Business success is founded on cocreation: creation of service experiences that build the customer's relationship with the organization, thereby creating cash flows to the organization. Customer experiences build strong relationships between an organization and its customers, creating customer loyalty and switching costs, which (in turn) makes the organization more effective and efficient. For example, Starbucks was able to achieve a financial turnaround in 2009 by leveraging these linkages. Innovations and improvements in Starbucks' service led to a more appealing customer experience, which revitalized relationships with potential and existing customers, thereby generating growth in sales. This chapter describes how to quantify the financial value of the customer relationship *to the organization*. It describes the principles of customer relationship management, an approach to managing how the organization relates to existing and potential customers.

Customer Lifetime Value

Customer lifetime value (CLV) is the sum of the discounted net contribution margins over time from all products purchased by the customer—that is, the revenue provided to the company less the company's cost associated with maintaining a relationship with the customer. CLV is calculated using a simple financial formula, which sums the organization's discounted cash flows from a single customer over T periods ($t = 1 \ldots T$).

$$CLV = \sum_{t=1}^{T} \frac{(GM_t)r^t}{(1+d)^t}$$

where GM_t represents the gross margin of all services purchased from a given customer during time period t, r represents the organizations retention rate expressed as a percentage, and d represents the organization's discount rate or cost of capital. In order to calculate gross margin at the customer level, the organization should to be able to sum all the products purchased by the customer during a time period. This information requirement poses challenges for organizations that serve the same customer through separate strategic business units. A customer's retention rate is related to the length of the relationship between a customer and the organization. The retention rate can be measured as the percentage of the total customer base that repurchases within a given time period or

Exhibit 5.1 Sample CLV Calculation

An auto dealership tracks customers who use its service facility. New customers represent \$50 in first-year margins, \$100 in second-year margins, \$125 in third-year margins, and \$100 in margins in subsequent years. The dealership estimates that customers defect at a rate of 20% per year. That is, only 80% of new customers continue to use the automobile dealership's services in the second year, only 60% of new customers continue to use the automobile dealership's services in the third year, and so on.

1. Using a 20% discount rate, calculate the "customer lifetime value" from these automobile service data:
   - Determine annual profit (or cash) flow for each year for a typical customer.
   - Establish customer defection pattern for each year.
   - Calculate the expected cash flow (after defections) for each year.

- Calculate the net present value of the cash flows using the firm's discount rate

2. Suppose that the dealership improves the customer experience so that customers defect at a rate of 15% a year instead of 20% of year. What is the new lifetime value of an average customer? How much should the dealership be willing to invest to improve service?

Solution

Year	Margin	Retention	Discount factor	Calculation
0	Assume no acquisition cost			
1	50	1.00	(1.2)	50 × 1/(1.2)
2	100	0.80	$(1.2)^2$	100 × 0.8/ $(1.2)^2$
3	125	0.60	$(1.2)^3$	125 × 0.6/ $(1.2)^3$
4	100	0.40	$(1.2)^4$	100 × 0.4/ $(1.2)^4$
5	100	0.20	$(1.2)^5$	100 × 0.2/ $(1.2)^5$
To answer question one, sum the values in the right column. The CLV is $167.95. To answer question two, conduct similar calculations. If the defection rate is 15% (i.e., the retention rate is 85%), the CLV becomes $205.10. The maximum you would be willing to pay (per customer) for an improvement that would reduce defections by 5% is equal to the change in the average lifetime value = $205.10 − $167.96 = $37.14				

as a probability that a particular customer will repurchase within a given time period.

Exhibit 5.1 shows a sample calculation for an auto-servicing company.[1] This example forecasts CLV under two scenarios. In the first scenario, the auto-servicing company continues its current actions and the CLV for the average customer is $167.96. Rather than making a calculation for an average customer, the auto-servicing company can make this calculation for each customer or group of customers—thereby identifying its most valuable customers and making targeted decisions about serving them. In the second scenario, the company considers undertaking some new initiatives to improve the customer experience and increase retention by 5 percent. The calculations show the CLV increases by $37.14 per customer. This number places an upper bound on how much the company should be willing to spend to improve the customer experience. Naturally, the company could calculate CLV for different customer groups under different scenarios (i.e., company actions) and decide which actions are most appropriate. This example illustrates that CLV calculations will always be *estimates* of future cash flows. Some questions to consider are as follows:

- What are the costs of acquiring a customer (advertising, sales force efforts, etc.)? What are the costs of retaining a customer (beyond the delivery of the experience)?
- Will there be decreases in operating costs as the company and customer know each other better?
- Are there word-of-mouth effects from satisfied customers? How can these be estimated?
- Are loyal customers more willing to pay a price premium?

Managers estimate gross margins and retention rates by analyzing the organization's customer records and making predictions about the future. If the records do not provide sufficient information, they can be estimated from survey data. At the individual customer level, the customer retention rate is the opposite of the customer's probability of switching to a competitor. It can be calculated as: probability of switching = (1 - probability of retention). Since it can be difficult to observe switching among competing service providers, switching probabilities are sometimes measured by surveying customers.[2]

Calculating CLV for each customer can be quite complex, but many organizations do so (or try to do so). Many organizations do not have customer records that show purchases across all products—often because they are sold by different strategic business units. Hence, the first and most difficult step is to unify and integrate all customer records—which can be very costly.

Case Study: Merrill Lynch Creates a Customer-Focused Account Platform

In 2013, Bank of America Merrill Lynch began a 12-month rollout of a $100 million project to merge its five separately managed account platforms into one. Their investment in technology enables a financial advisor to have complete view of their clients' accounts, so that they can efficiently supervise assets and provide improved guidance to clients. Not all firms need to make such large investments, but many will need to adjust their record-keeping. It is necessary to create individual customer records that show all products purchased over time and estimate customer defection rates over time.

CLV predictions should be based on forecasts of revenue sources and costs to serve—given a particular set of organizational actions, competitor actions, and market conditions. Hence, although CLV is often considered a fixed value, different forecasts are possible under different scenarios. It is a prediction that is influenced by (and influences) the organization's strategy. Predictions about CLV should take into account whether the organization or its competitors' activities will change over time, as well as changes in the business environment.

In addition to CLV, there are many other metrics that organizations use to manage their service operations, such as number of acquired customers, "churn" as a percentage of the customer base, and the dollar value of cross-selling. A study compared CLV measures with RFM (**R**ecency, **F**requency, **M**onetary value) and PCV (**P**ast **C**ustomer **V**alue). It showed that CLV was better at predicting the future profitability of a customer.[3] When interpreting these metrics, it is important to remember that the organization should allocate its resources based on forecasts of the customer's *future* profitability, and not his or her current or past profitability. For example, a college-educated consumer in her midtwenties (holding few financial products) will have a longer cash flow stream than an older consumer currently holding more products. The predicted length of the relationship, as well as the number of products the consumer is likely to hold, will influence future profitability.

Customer relationship management seeks to increase revenues, profits, and firm value through strategies that develop, maintain, and enhance successful company–customer relationships.[4] It aligns customer and organization goals, as well as manages the customer experience and relationship over time. It usually uses systems, information technology, and people to design and deliver excellent customer experiences that build relationships as sources of value.

Point to Ponder: Should managers consider service "costs" a current accounting cost or a long-term investment?

Customer Retention: The Math Tells a Story

Based on the CLV formula, there are three ways to increase CLV and (consequently) the organization's cash flows:

1. The organization can increase the lifetime of the customer—that is, increase the probability that the customer stays in the relationship, called the customer retention rate.
2. The organization can find ways to increase the gross margins obtained from the customer—that is, by encouraging the customer to use more products (goods or services) or purchase higher margin services. These strategies might include changing the portfolio of services offered by the firm.
3. The organization can acquire more customers, perhaps through additional sales efforts, thereby increasing the size of the customer base.

At this point, it is useful to note that—for most companies—increasing customer retention will have the most powerful effect on CLV and (hence) cash flows.[5] Small increases in retention rates can have a dramatic effect on the profits of a company because the cost of retaining an existing customer is usually much less than that of acquiring a new customer, existing customers tend to purchase more than new customers and there are efficiencies in dealing with existing customers rather than new customers.[6] The following case study will suffice to demonstrate this point.

Case Study: A Cellular Phone Provider in the United States

In the early 1990s, cellular communications providers in the United States had very high "churn" rates (i.e., customer turnover rates), often 35 percent per year or higher. What does this statistic tell us? It means that the "lifetime" or duration of the relationship with the average customer was about three years! With a 35 percent defection rate, the existing customer base vanishes in three years. Each provider tried to offset customer defections by aggressively acquiring new customers—often by targeting their competitors' customers. However, this strategy was very expensive. Managers eventually realized that a better solution was to reduce the churn rate.

If the churn rate was decreased to 20 percent, the existing customer base would fall more slowly. The average lifetime of a customer would be about five years. At that time, the average customer's phone bill was about $50 per month. A rough calculation that ignores the time value of money or discount rate is the following. If churn is 35 percent, the average CLV is roughly ($50 per month × 12 months × 3 years =) $1,800. If churn is 20 percent, the average CLV is roughly ($50 per month × 12 months × 5 years =) $3,000. The difference is $1200. Multiplying by the size of the cellular provider's existing customer base, the payoff to reducing churn—that is, increasing customer retention—was huge. Over time, cellular communications providers moved to a new business model that featured fixed-period service contracts and premium service packages with usage fees (e.g., data services). A similar phenomenon is now taking place in the entertainment and media industries.

Once they understand CLV, most managers realize that increasing customer retention is extremely important. What are some ways to reduce churn? As discussed in Chapter 1, organization should design and deliver superior customer experiences, so that customer relationships are enhanced and customers stay longer. Why? Customers who are more satisfied with their experience have longer relationships with the service organization than customers who are less satisfied.[7] Moreover, the influence of satisfaction on relationship length is more pronounced when the customer is more experienced with the service organization.[8]

How to Use CLV in Making Decisions

There are two important ways that CLV helps in making decisions:

1. CLV helps identify the customers that the organization wants to serve.
2. CLV helps organizations get the most out of all its customers.

First, the organization's ability to calculate the lifetime value of each customer helps it answer the question: which customers does the organization want to serve? Many organizations discover that a small percentage of its most profitable customers (say, the top 20 percent) account for the vast majority of its profits (say 80 percent). This discovery leads to the natural question. How can the organization better serve its most profitable customers? In addition, organizations often discover that some customers cost money, time, and effort but do not provide appropriate returns. If these customers can't be made profitable, the organization will usually decide to allocate fewer resources to them.

Second, CLV helps organizations "get the most" out of all its customers.[9] Organizations can group customers according to their long-run profitability and offer differentiated experiences to each group.[10] The organization's goal should be to discover groups of customers who have similar preferences for service—and then serve them in customized ways that increase their profitability. As a rule of thumb, investments in service improvements and innovations are warranted when they cost less than the resultant increase in CLV. The strategic components of a market-oriented strategy are: market segmentation, target marketing, and positioning. The inputs to these managerial decisions are an analysis of the market, customers, and competitors. For example, the "Balanced Scorecard" calls for executive level management to routinely monitor and evaluate customer knowledge, internal business processes, learning and growth—as well as financial performance.[11]

Customer Equity

Customer equity is the long-run value of the organization's existing *and potential* customers, in aggregate. It can be considered an estimate of the long-run value of a firm. One way to calculate customer equity is to calculate CLV at the level of the individual or market segment, and then aggregate across customers and potential customers.[12] When disaggregate information about customers is not available, it is sometimes possible to estimate customer equity using publicly available information from a firm's financial statements. Scholars have used such information from annual reports to calculate the (post-tax) customer-based value of five companies and found that their estimates were reasonably close to the reported market values (i.e., value for shareholders) for three firms, but significantly lower for two Internet firms, Amazon and eBay.[13] The market values for the internet firms were higher because analysts were predicting additional sources of cash flows.

Early interest in customer equity arose because managers wanted to know how best to allocate spending on customer acquisition activities versus retention activities to maximize the organization's cash flows and, consequently, market value.[14] Most organization seek to grow, so managers tend to focus on acquiring new customers. However, customer retention typically has the largest influence (vis-à-vis other components) on the value of the customer base.[15] The reason for this discrepancy is that organizations haven't measured customer defections and their associated costs.

Most managers begin by thinking that retaining 80 percent of their customers is "good"—until they realize that this retention rate implies that all their existing customers will have defected in five or six years. Instead, an 80 percent customer retention rate suggests the organization can be compared to a sink without a stopper. You may turn on the tap (i.e., acquire customers), but the sink doesn't fill up (i.e., the customer base doesn't expand). Customers are continuously leaving and must be replaced—which erodes the organization's profitability—because customers are not replaced as easily as turning on a tap. Even small increases in customer retention (say, 5 percent) substantially increase the organization's cash flows from customers over time. Thus, surprisingly, increases in customer retention can be a source of organic growth!

Moreover, since customer acquisition is typically more expensive than customer retention activities, the organization also benefits from reduced expenditures to attract new customers.[16] For example, some mobile communications organizations give a customer a "free cell phone" when she signs a two-year contract for service. The organization will recover the cost of the phone—and more—as the customer pays for voice and data services over the next two years. The key takeaway regarding customer equity is quite straightforward. Service improvement and innovation strategies provide different avenues for creating excellent customer experiences, thereby building strong relationships between organizations and their customers. These efforts increase competitive advantage and (ultimately) customer equity. Hence, service innovation and improvement in customer experiences "pay off" in three ways: customer acquisition, increases in customer retention and improvements in contribution margins.

Up until now, this chapter has focused on customer relationship management to increase the cash flow stream from an individual customer or market segment (group of customers who respond in similar ways to organizational actions). Now, let us consider the implications of managing CLV for *all* potential and existing customers.

Managing the Customer Portfolio

An organization's relationships with its customers can be considered "market-based assets" that an organization continuously invests in, in order to be viable in the marketplace.[17] This viewpoint suggests that the principles of managing financial portfolios can be applied to the management of customer portfolios. One approach to identifying service strategies that create excellent customer experiences and durable relationships is to decompose CLV into its underlying sources—customer acquisition, retention, and margin—which are amenable to managerial action. Each is a source of organic growth.

Organizations can increase customer equity by acquiring and retaining customers who create the largest cash flows—guided by measures of CLV and the customer's perception of the service experience. For existing customers, organizations can increase service usage, service upgrades, and the purchase of additional services. They can also improve their overall profitability by adjusting prices, managing costs, and adjusting their service offerings. Since not all customers are equally profitable, resources should be allocated to customers based on their future (not current) profit potential. These strategies require the organization to develop programs targeted at individual customers or segments to increase customer equity by influencing:

- Customer acquisition;
- Customer retention; and
- Margins (through targeting high-value customers or cross-selling or both).

There are a number of different approaches to identify programs or projects that will influence these three components. They have been well described in the business press.[18] This chapter summarizes the key principles underlying them.

Customer Acquisition

Converting prospects to customers can be expensive and challenging.[19] Organizations with a reputation for a superior customer experience will generate favorable comparisons with competitors and positive word-of-mouth; hence, they are likely to find it easier to acquire new customers. However, as discussed in Chapter 4, product-customer fit is key. Targeting, acquiring, and keeping the "right" customers entails a consideration of their fit with current service offerings, their future profitability and contribution to overall business risk. Some organizations inadvertently recruit customers who are not profitable—so customer acquisition can be a costly and risky process. Also, if new customers are not a good fit with the organization's value proposition, the organization may alter its competitive positioning in the marketplace or alienate existing customers or both. In other words, customer acquisition can influence the diversity of the customer portfolio, thereby influencing business risk.

Customer Retention

Customer retention is often easier and cheaper than customer acquisition, especially in stable markets, with low growth rates. An organizational emphasis on customer retention also makes sense when discount rates are low,[20] as they have been recently in the United States. Customers who have higher satisfaction levels and better price perceptions have longer relationships with organizations. In other words, satisfaction and favorable price perceptions provides "insulation" from the competition. For these reasons, Chapter 4 devoted considerable attention to how people for their assessments of satisfaction and price. However, customer retention and defection are complex processes—which is why the ability of service strategies to create bonds between organizations and their customers is so important. For this reason, Chapter 7 discusses how organizations can recover from a failure to deliver an excellent service experience. The following case study of how Starbucks has met challenges to growth

Case Study: Starbucks Invests in the Customer Experience

In 2008, Starbucks' customer satisfaction ratings, operating income—and share price—dropped substantially, causing Howard Schultz to return as CEO. A major reason for the drop in customer satisfaction ratings was that the company had grown very quickly. The mix of customers had changed. Many new customers were attracted to Starbucks' coffee experience, but they also wanted fast customer service. Growth challenged the ability of baristas to provide personal service, customized drinks, and serve many customers quickly.

Under Schultz's leadership, the company cut costs by millions of dollars—especially focusing on supply chain efficiencies and "right sizing" the organization (which included some store closings). Most cost-cutting did not involve consumer-facing activities. At the same time, Starbucks invested in service innovations (technology and stored value cards) and in its people. Specifically, it added staff hours at each coffee house to restore the quality of its customer service and increase its speed in serving customers. For example, in 2010, Starbucks retrained its baristas to slow down. Instead of grinding beans at the beginning of the day, baristas returned to grinding coffee beans fresh for each batch and handling only one or two customized drinks at any time.

Schultz's rationale was that changing the baristas' behavior would create a more consistent coffee experience—and more satisfied customers. Slowly, ratings of customer satisfaction with the coffee experience began to rise. Their service strategies were important in attracting and retaining Starbucks customers who appreciated the improved service experience and visited Starbucks frequently. Customer acquisition, retention, and frequency of visits (which affects margins) rose. In subsequent years, Starbucks resumed its growth and profitability.

provides a useful example of how service strategies can increase retention and the value of the customer portfolio.[21]

This case study also reinforces an important point. There is no service strategy or competitive advantage that is sustainable in the long run. "The ability to learn faster than competitors may be the only true sustainable competitive advantage."[22] Starbucks' customers' preferences had changed; its competitors had changed. Starbucks was forced to learn, adapt, and innovate. By doing so, it was able to create customer experiences to build relationships—and that led to increased cash flows. As markets change, organizations must be attentive and willing to pursue service improvements and innovation in order to sustain a competitive advantage.

Gross Margins

Organizations can increase CLV and gross margin per customer by encouraging the purchase of premium products. The organization's capabilities and resources will play an important role in determining the effectiveness of its cross-selling activities. Not surprisingly, customers who have had excellent service experiences with the organization in the past are more likely to increase their usage of an organization's services and buy additional services—especially when they fit their needs.[23]

Although organizations may have customers who are unprofitable to serve ("free riders"), firing customers or refusing to serve them is seldom necessary. Instead, organizations can offer a different value proposition to some segments, such as by raising prices or adjusting the service offering. Another option is to find a way to make customers more profitable by changing the organization's business model. For example, IBM wanted to focus on *Fortune* 1,000 companies, but could not ignore less profitable relationships with small business. Hence, they developed a dealer network that could serve the medium and small businesses in a profitable way.

***Point to Ponder*:** From a financial standpoint, does it make sense for an organization to fire unprofitable customers? How (in practice) might a company carry out this policy? Are there ways to migrate customers to channels where cost-to-serve is low? Are there ways to create no-frills offerings that appeal to them?

Optimizing the Customer Portfolio or Mix

A customer portfolio can be viewed analogously to a financial portfolio, where the organization's goal is to maximize returns for a given level of risk. What is the risk in a customer portfolio? Each customer or market segment can be considered an asset with a stream of unpredictable future cash flows. Customer risk originates from different sources of variability in cash inflows and outflows, arising from customer defection, product usage, cross-buying, customer characteristics, competitive effects, and firm actions.[24] Hence, whenever the organization makes decisions about which customers to acquire, retain, or divest, it is altering the overall characteristics of the customer portfolio.[25] This implies that organizations *cannot* maximize customer equity by independently maximizing the CLV of individual customers or market segments. The organization must consider how different cash flow streams complement each other and contribute to the aggregate cash flow stream.

Experts have warned that "when analyzing the forest rather than the trees, weaker customer relationships, judged unprofitable on a CLV basis, may, over time, actually create value as a part of a broader portfolio."[26] In other words, focusing on the magnitude of cash flow from customers (i.e., expected returns) reveals only half of the story. Managers need to understand the influence of customers on the volatility and variability of cash flows over time. Thus, both returns (CLV) and risk (variance) of cash flows are relevant to customer portfolio decisions.

Similar to the principles for managing a financial portfolio, the organization should manage the customer portfolio to achieve returns commensurate to the risk it is willing to assume. In other words, decisions about individual customers cannot be made without considering its effects on the cash flow stream of the entire customer portfolio.[27] Organizations can increase shareholder value by structuring a customer portfolio to reduce the vulnerability and volatility of cash flows—without sacrificing returns or decreasing customer equity. Scholars have demonstrated how to optimize the customer portfolio for B2B organizations (a logistics firm) and B2C organizations (financial services and telecommunications),[28] but the methodology is new, so it has not been widely adopted yet. However, the basic principles are quite straightforward, as the following case illustrates.

Case Study: IBM Successfully Manages Its Customer Portfolio

Large corporations were battered by the financial recession that affected the European Union during 2000 to 2001 and the United States in 2002 to 2003. IBM's portfolio of customers included large *Fortune* 500 customers; these customers can be considered the equivalent of blue-chip stocks. IBM derived recurring revenue streams from multiyear outsourcing contracts from other large organizations, resembling a triple-A-rated bond. However, IBM also served a mix of small and medium-sized companies, characterized by higher volatility and growth—rather like small-cap stocks—as well as a host of international customers. Its balanced portfolio shielded IBM from the severe volatility that characterized the IT sector during 2008 to 2009.

In contrast, some of IBM's competitors, such as Sun Microsystems Inc., overweighted their customer portfolio toward dot-com companies in the late 1990s. Consequently, Sun experienced extreme volatility in earnings during the early 2000s. Bankruptcy hit many of the startups that had provided a dominant source of its revenue—which in turn affected Sun's cash flows. (Sun was acquired by Oracle Corporation in 2010.)

More generally, by considering the complementarity or similarity of market segments, an organization can weigh the composition of the customer portfolio to ensure that its risk-adjusted return meets organizational objectives. The general idea is that decreases in cash flows from one market segment should be offset by increases in cash flows from another market segment, so that the aggregate cash flow of the organization remains stable over time. For example, B2B organizations often choose to serve a mix of small and large customers (rather than focusing only on large customers) because the cash flow patterns of the two segments offset each other during periods when the national economy expands or contracts. Service strategies provide opportunities to allocate resources to market segments to achieve these objectives. They also help design consistent processes (with less variability in service operations) that are cost-effective and create excellent customer experiences.

A recent study has shown that *variability* in individual customers' consumption or spending can be decreased in ways that are actionable by most organizations, without decreasing revenues or profits.[29] These findings were robust across two settings: telecommunications and financial services, and across customer segments. The study identified four ways to increase cash flow levels and variability:

1. An increase in customer satisfaction has a "double-whammy" effect: lower cash flow variability and higher cash flow levels.
2. Customers who participate in loyalty programs have more variable cash flows, but not higher average cash flows. Hence, firms should design loyalty programs to improve customer satisfaction or intangible benefits (e.g., membership recognition), rather than offering economic incentives.
3. Customers who purchase many different offerings or allocate a large share of their purchases to the firm, have higher cash flow variability and higher average cash flows. Thus, organizations can optimize the customer portfolio by combining customers with high variability with customers who have different, offsetting cash flow patterns.
4. Consumer characteristics, such as age and income, also influence cash flow variability. In the same way, firmographics also influence cash flow variability.[30] Hence, organizations can manage cash flow levels and variability through careful attention to market segmentation strategies.

Higher variability in cash flows is acceptable only when there are commensurate returns in the form of higher cash flow levels. For this reason, these findings provide useful guidelines to managers concerning ways to reduce cash flow variability without adversely affecting cash flow levels by better managing the customer experience.

Monetizing the Customer Experience

Until this point, this chapter has discussed how to manage the customer experience to optimize customer equity without specifically addressing a key organizational challenge: pricing strategies and tactics. Monetizing the customer experience has become somewhat bewildering due to the complexities of the modern business landscape. For example, after introducing a paywall in 2011, the *New York Times* reached one million digital subscribers in 2015. Yet, other newspapers have struggled to find a successful business model, and many observers had predicted that this feat was impossible. How was it successful? The *Times* offers different digital subscription options for different platforms: web, smartphone, tablet, and multiplatform. It also generates revenues from traditional paper subscribers, advertisers, and other sources. This anecdote illustrates some of the opportunities and challenges of monetizing the customer experience. There are many ways to price products, including usage-based pricing, price bundles, and price tiers.

Pricing decisions typically have a larger effect on customer demand than any other managerial decision variable. Why? Recall that the lifetime value of a customer is the (expected) net present value of all future profits generated from a customer. A simple approach to estimating CLV has been proposed by Gupta and Lehmann.[31]

CLV = margin (retention rate/[1 + discount rate – retention rate])[32]

This equation provides a quick and easy way to estimate the CLV for a "typical" customer in one market segment. Managers can add up CLV across customers and segments to obtain an estimate of the dollar value of the customer base.[33] Managers have only two "levers" to increase cash flows from *existing* customers. They can increase margins or increase customer retention, where both are influenced by price. Margins are higher when prices are higher, unit costs lower or both. In particular, margins are higher when an organization acquires customers who are willing to pay a premium for service and can be migrated to higher price or higher margin services or encouraged to buy additional services. Retention rates are higher when the organization designs and delivers a customer experience that is superior to competitors at a competitive price.

Customers who are satisfied with their experience are likely to return and buy additional services,[34] which leads to a focus on delivering high quality service experiences at the most attractive price. To simplify a complex topic, the following discussion focuses on four issues:

1. Key pricing factors
2. Price fairness
3. Pricing and service usage
4. Price tiers

Point to Ponder: Financial services, such as banks and insurance companies, have quickly adopted sophisticated customer portfolio management and pricing practices. Do other organizations have the ability to track customer behavior over time, calculate retention rates, and estimate profit margins for each product in each market segment (or for each individual customer)?

Key Pricing Factors

Based on economic principles, an organization's pricing decision should depend on three key factors:

- The benefits of the customer experience.
- The benefits and prices of competitors' offerings.
- The costs of creating and delivering the service experience.

The benefits of the customer experience create a "price ceiling," sometimes called the customer's reservation price or willingness to pay. The reservation price is the maximum that customers will pay for a service experience. It will depend on the availability of substitutes, the extent to which the service experience is differentiated from competitors, brand reputation, and switching costs. The cost of designing and delivering the service experience is the "price floor." This cost is the minimum that the organization must receive to cover all fixed and variable costs. The range between the price ceiling and the price floor is the "pricing latitude" available to the organization. The organization's ability to charge a price within this range depends on customers' sensitivity to price changes, as well as the service experiences and prices of competitors.

Excellent customer experiences provide opportunities to differentiate the organization's offering and provide more pricing latitude within this range. Since customers are characterized by different lifetime values and perceptions of the competing service experiences, the organization may employ different service and pricing strategies for different groups of customers. In addition, the organization can think outside the box and try to raise the price ceiling—that is, find ways to deliver more benefits to customers—or lower the price floor—that is, find ways to drive down costs.

Price Fairness

How does the organization find the optimal price point? A significant consideration is whether the customer perceives the price to be fair. One reason for the popularity of eBay and Priceline.com is that these auction services allow buyers to pay exactly the price that they currently consider "fair" in return for the benefits they receive. Given how customers form their expectations, it is likely that customers will compare the organization's price for the service experience with past prices or the prices of competitors. In the same way, a manager should consider the price of similar services offered by competitors.

Price fairness can be roughly evaluated by comparing the experience per dollar of each competing service, by making the following comparison:

$$\text{Experience}_A/\text{Price}_A > = < \text{Experience}_B/\text{Price}_B$$

(The subscript denotes the competing firms, A and B.) In this equation, "experience" refers to the customer's assessment of the design and delivery of the customer's experience in a given context at a particular point in time (as depicted in Figure 4.1). The organization's goal is to ensure that customers perceive its experience–price ratio to be more favorable than competitors' ratios. A useful way for managers to identify their competitors is to study how customers substitute services in actual usage situations.

A simple example can explain why these analyses are helpful. Kayla works out at the fitness center several times a week at Gym A; the cost is $25 per week. Her friends tell her that nearby Gym B offers equivalent facilities and services at the same price. However, many of her friends are currently taking a yoga class at Gym B; Kayla looks at some photos on Instagram and they are having a lot of fun. From Kayla's point of view, Gym B is providing a better customer experience: $Experience_B/P_B > Experience_A/P_A$, so she switches to Gym B for social and emotional reasons.

This calculation highlights that—from an organizational standpoint—the *best* customer experience is not necessarily the *highest* quality offering when quality is defined from a product-focused, rather than a customer-focused viewpoint. From Kayla's viewpoint, the two gyms are roughly equivalent in terms of facilities and services. However, she decides to switch gyms for social and emotional reasons generated by online C2C activities. The design and delivery of the customer experience should depend on how much customers in the target market are willing to pay for different aspects of the experience. Organizations will have many market segments, where each responds differently to elements of the customer experience. Note that a separate evaluation must be made for each customer or segment because their experiences will be different.

Case Study: Value Place Rethinks the Extended-Stay Hotel Experience

Value Place, a new entrant into the extended-stay hotel market, competes by delivering low prices, guaranteed cleanliness and safety, and a consistent brand experience at every property. A room costs roughly $159 to 249 *per week*, with minimal amenities and free housekeeping service provided every 14 days or upon checkout. Its target market includes travelers who are paying their own way or business travelers on tight per diem budgets or who continually travel. This market segment evaluates the design and delivery of the customer experience at Value Place to be more favorable than (say) a Marriott Residence Inn given their comparative prices. Value Place expanded rapidly with 500 new franchise commitments in 2004 to 2006, and average occupancy rates above 90 percent.[35]

There are opportunities for the organization to actively manage customers' perceptions of price fairness through communications that influence expectations.

- Many organizations set a reference (a list or "regular" price) so that customers will make upward comparisons. However, managers should be careful not to create a reference price that is unsustainable—such as a too-low market penetration price or a too-high marking skimming price. For example, Apple initially set a too-high price for its iPhone 6 and—as demand was weak—then rapidly reduced its price.
- Organizations should encourage favorable comparisons with other offerings. For example, car-sharing services have recently emerged in the European marketplace. Their prices compare favorably with taxis over short distances and with solo travel (due to high petrol prices). In some instances, it may be necessary for organizations to differentiate their service experience to discourage unwanted comparisons. For example, Southwest Airlines advertises that passengers can check two pieces of luggage for free when other airlines are charging for checked luggage.
- Organizations sometimes offer different prices to different groups of customers when the costs of serving them are different. If so, managers should be mindful that people make social comparisons. They may ask: is it fair that airline passengers are offered a discount if they book in advance? Is it fair that business customers have a special waiting line at the bank (that moves much faster)? In these situations, people usually

decide that it is fair for organizations to offer different prices. However, other situations are much less clear-cut. When customers can observe that people pay different prices, the organization may need to communicate why prices are lower for some market segments than others.

Pricing and Service Usage

Customers' perceptions of price fairness are also influenced by a comparison of their *usage* and *payment* levels (i.e., the size of their bill) with what they expected.[36] For example, a consumer with a fitness club membership is likely to perceive the price as unfair when she does not use the facilities very often (a comparison of actual and expected usage levels). Or, a cellular phone customer is likely to perceive the price as unfair when she sees an unexpectedly large bill. From this perspective, it makes sense for the organization to encourage usage so that payment levels seem fair—or to migrate customers to a price plan that better fits their usage pattern. (After, even if the consumer's monthly bill is lower, she may stay longer!)

Many organizations segment the market on the basis of service usage (e.g., heavy versus light users), implicitly assuming that customer usage levels are relatively stable. Yet, research highlights that usage varies; it is a decision the customer makes on the basis of his or her experiences with the service provider.[37] Customers appear to manage usage to maintain "fair" payment levels and cumulative satisfaction in the service relationship. These findings yield several useful implications for managers.

- Organizations should be proactive in helping customers maintain payment fairness and satisfaction. They might consider customizing service bundles, helping customers migrate to more attractive price plans, and so forth. A common concern of managers is that they are "leaving money on the table." However, failure to proactively manage the customer relationship may cause customers to exit from the relationship with the service organization and switch to a competitor's products.

- Managers should weigh the effects of pricing policy on perceptions of payment fairness, satisfaction, and future usage when setting prices for continuously provided services. If price increases are likely to lead to decreases in payment equity, organizations may be able to introduce pricing plans that increase (net) overall satisfaction and usage of the service—thereby maintaining or enhancing profitability.
- There are significant differences in the impact of price and price changes for fixed price and two-part pricing services, which suggests that pricing strategies may play an important role in long-term customer satisfaction, usage, and loyalty. Although there are highly sophisticated models of the effect of price on short-run behavior (e.g., trial or choice behavior), managers to date have paid much less attention to the effect of price on long-run behavior with respect to continuously provided services. As the anecdote about the *New York Times* suggests, organizations may need to consider diverse fixed and usage-based pricing plans that match customers' different circumstances.
- To manage customer relationships more effectively, organizations must understand and anticipate:
  - Customers' reactions to the organization's actions (changes in price, marketing communications, or the experience itself); and
  - Customers' reactions to their own decisions and actions (usage levels, fairness comparisons).

Price Tiers

Most organizations sell more than one offering, so they must consider how to price the entire product line. When products are complements, organizations may choose to bundle products and services. From the customer's standpoint, bundles may better match their needs than a large menu of items. From the organization's standpoint, bundling allows them to capture value from customers who have different reservation prices for different components of the bundle. Customers must practice a certain amount of mental accounting to identify suitable bundles and then compare competing offerings.

Many information technology companies derive a substantial portion of their revenues from selling services, cloud computing, business solutions, and consulting to their customers (who are sometimes called their "installed base"). These companies are adopting a customer-focused, service-centric view. They are developing new services based on the analysis and interpretation of their business customer's data. At both Siemens and IBM, business analytics enabled them to design and deliver services that reduce system downtime, thereby improving the consistency of the customer experience. As data has migrated from customer-owned servers to The Cloud, both companies have moved to revenue models based on tiered service contracts, where the fees are based on performance levels (downtime) that are directly connected to the customer experience. Both companies provide information about system performance to business customers through a web portal, thereby providing tangible signals of the quality of the service experience.

Technology has led to the unbundling of many services and the disintermediation of other services. In addition, organizations must recognize that customers can, and do, create their own bundles.

Case Study: Disintermediation and Unbundling in the Entertainment Industry

Consumers are canceling their subscriptions to traditional pay television services—especially cable and satellite service. They are moving to new digital distribution outlets such as online streaming and mobile, where they can watch some of the same shows via Netflix and Hulu. To slow down customer defections, cable and satellite services are offering smaller, less expensive bundles of channels. In addition, premium services such as HBO and Showtime have introduced stand-alone services outside traditional cable subscriptions. Despite these efforts, lower customer retention rates for cable and satellite subscriptions are having ripple effects—lowering cash flows for media companies such as Disney, 21st Century Fox, and Time Warner.[38]

All of these service organizations, distributors, and media companies have been forced to rethink their business models, including their license fees from Netflix and Hulu. In addition, CBS has announced a streaming service for its broadcast service that would not require a traditional cable subscription. Changes in how people consume entertainment services (unbundled rather than bundled services) are completely changing customer retention rates for established companies and reshaping the entertainment and media sectors.

A common and useful practice is to create tiered value options. B2B service contracts usually have low-, medium-, and high-value options, where each contract type has different levels of design quality, experience quality, and price. These options are somewhat substitutable, but they are intended to correspond to different customer needs, ranging from a need for upon-request service only (i.e., low value) to customized, fast, and proactive service (i.e., high value). By designing and selling these service contracts, the organization's goal is to match customers with the product that best fits their need to maximize customer–product fit and create an excellent customer experience. For example, Hewlett Packard Enterprise offers system support contracts for servers operated by very large enterprises. Its high-value service contracts are intended for companies that use their servers in "mission critical" areas, such as customer-facing activities. These contracts usually cover a period of time (say, three years), where contract descriptions and terms help clarify and align the goals and expectations for both parties. During this time period, the contract specifications help keep the relationship on track.

***Point to Ponder*:** In the offline world, desirable customers may have their fees waived and get other hidden discounts based on the value of their business. Less valuable customers may never even know the promotions exist. Under what circumstances are such practices fair? Feasible?

Key Ideas

- CLV is a forecast of the future net cash flows from a customer based on assumptions about the firm's future actions and the business environment.
- Forecasts of CLV can help organizations identify which customers to serve and how to serve them—to get the most out of each customer.
- The CLV equation shows that all growth strategies operate through three levers that can increase cash flow:
    - Customer acquisition
    - Retention
    - Margins
- For most organizations, an increase in customer retention is the most powerful pathway to increasing cash flows and reducing their variability over time. High retention levels not only increase cash flows from existing customers but also increase efficiencies in attracting and serving customers.
- Organizations should manage their customer mix so that the cash flows of individual customers complement each other over time—that is, peaks and valleys offset each other—so that returns are the same (or higher) and cash flow variability or risk is lower.
- An organization can charge a premium vis-à-vis a competitor if it delivers a superior customer experience (when all benefits are considered) per dollar. Organizations should look for ways to develop pricing latitude, as well as considering tiered offerings.
- Many factors influence price perceptions and judgments about price fairness, so an organization must work to create favorable comparisons, align expectations, and reinforce quality signals concerning the customer experience.
- A common and useful practice is to create tiered value options. By designing and selling tiered options (good, better, best), the organization's goal is to match customers with the product that best fits their need to maximize customer–product fit and create an excellent customer experience.

Notes

1. We have simplified the defection calculations. In year three, we show the defection rate as 0.80 - 0.20 = 0.60. However, a precise calculation is 0.80 × 0.80 = 0.64. (In year four, it would be [0.80 × 0.80 × 0.80 = 0.512].) The calculations can become even more complex. For example, defection rates can differ over time or across customers. It is necessary to track customers over time to discover your customers' defection rates.
2. Rust, Lemon, and Zeithaml (2004).
3. Venkatesan and Kumar (2004).
4. Berry (1983, 25); Grőnroos (1990); Morgan and Hunt (1994, 22).
5. Payne and Rickard (1997); Reichheld (1996).
6. Fornell and Wernerfelt (1987); Reichheld and Sasser (1990).
7. Bolton (1998); Boulding et al. (1993); Crosby and Stephens (1987).
8. Bolton (1998).
9. Thomas, Reinartz, and Kumar (2004).
10. Payne and Frow (2005).
11. Kaplan and Norton (2005).
12. Blattberg, Getz, and Thomas (2001).
13. Gupta, Lehmann, and Stuart (2004).
14. Blattberg and Deighton (1996).
15. Gupta (2009); Gupta et al. (2006).
16. Reichheld and Sasser (1990).
17. Srivastava, Shevani, and Fahey (1998).
18. Blattberg, Getz, and Thomas (2001); Gupta and Lehmann (2005); Rust, Lemon, and Zeithaml (2004); Tarasi et al. (2011, 2013).
19. Reinartz, Thomas, and Kumar (2005).
20. Gupta and Lehmann (2005).
21. Schultz and Gordon (2011).
22. De Geus (1988).
23. Bolton, Lemon, and Verhoef (2008).
24. Bolton and Tarasi (2015).
25. Johnson and Selnes (2004).
26. Johnson and Selnes (2004).
27. Dhar and Glazer (2003).
28. Tarasi et al. (2011, 2013).

29. Tarasi et al. (2013).
30. Tarasi et al. (2011).
31. Gupta and Lehmann (2005).
32. They make (and justify) three assumptions: (1) profit margins remain constant over the life of the customer, (2) retention rate for customers stays constant over time, and (3) customer lifetime value is calculated over an infinite time horizon.
33. The discount rate is a function of the organization's cost of capital and depends on its business risk and debt-equity structure.
34. Bolton, Lemon, and Verhoef (2004).
35. Sharkey (2006).
36. Bolton and Lemon (1999).
37. Bolton and Lemon (1999).
38. Steel (2015).

CHAPTER 6

Customer-Focused Innovation

Organizations are keenly interested in innovation as a source of organic growth and profitability. For this reason, they are adopting new approaches to identifying opportunities for innovation in business models, processes, and products. A variety of approaches are helpful for developing radical (i.e., large-scale) innovations, incremental innovations, and improvements. However, there are many challenges facing service organizations: the unique characteristics of the customer experience (intangibility, heterogeneity, simultaneity of production and consumption, perishability), changes in the business landscape that create new opportunities for service (advances in technology, new media), and the changing nature of customer participation in the creation and delivery of service. However, each organization will face different opportunities and challenges. Hence, this chapter will describe six principles to guide customer-focused innovation:

1. Adapting the stage-gate innovation process to incorporate the customer experience
2. Positioning offerings along the service infusion continuum
3. Identifying gaps in creating an excellent customer experience
4. Service blueprinting
5. Critical incident analysis and root cause analysis
6. Benchmarking

In addition, many organizations seek ways to generate customer-driven improvements from big data. The improvement process starts by managers understanding the service experience from the customer's point of view. There are three major sources of data about the customer experience available within the organization: engineering and operational measures generated by business systems and processes (e.g., hardware and software), social media data, and customer survey data. In an ideal world, organizations will create a unified database that matches all three sources at the level of the individual customer. However, they are often analyzed separately. Each of these sources has strengths and limitations. Hence, this chapter also describes several different ways to generate data-driven insights from existing information sources to identify improvements in the customer experience, including:

1. Key process indicators (KPIs)
2. Business analytics
3. Surveys
4. Dashboards and multiple metrics

It closes with some suggested next steps that should apply to every organization that seeks to improve the customer experience.

Changing the Stage-Gate Process for Service Innovation

For manufactured goods, there is a well-accepted stage-gate process for generating new ideas and bringing them to market.[1] This process includes distinct stages: market opportunity analysis, idea creation, concept development, business analysis and planning, prototype development (with refinement of pricing plans), and commercialization in the marketplace. At each stage, new ideas are rigorously evaluated and refined, so that only the best ideas proceed through the "gate" to the next stage. Specific techniques have been developed, such as conjoint analysis (for new concepts) and rapid-prototyping, to evaluate, refine, and test new ideas. A recent review of many studies shows that customer participation in the new product development process leads to better business outcomes.[2]

The stage-gate process has been widely used because it has been extremely successful at bringing new manufactured goods to market. Some experts have questioned whether it can be applied to service experiences without significant adaptation.[3] The stage-gate process may need to be changed in three ways:

1. Customers should be involved in almost every stage of the new product development process, especially the early (i.e., idea creation and concept development) and late (commercialization) stages.
2. The development of innovations in the customer experience must be protected from too early or inappropriate application of the gates or financial hurdles.
3. Small-scale, rapid, iterative testing of innovations in the customer experience may be appropriate at the commercialization stage.

***Point to Ponder*:** Why is it more difficult to conduct research and development (R&D) for customer experiences? Are there ways to bring customers into the R&D laboratory? To go out to the customer?

First, since customers participate in service experiences, many experts believe that customers must meaningfully participate in new product development for the innovation process to be successful. In other words, service innovation processes must be human-focused and harness people's creativity in cocreating the service experience over time. The available scholarly evidence suggests that customer participation is especially *important in the early and late stages of new product development*. There are many new technologies and research methods that rely on observation (rather than surveys), such as:

- Qualitative techniques, such as netnography and anthropology, can be used to better understand customer needs in a social context;
- Eye-tracking devices can be used to study people's responses to the store environment;
- Functional magnetic resonance imaging can be used to study how people respond to brands and advertising images[4];
- RFID technology can be used to track merchandise throughout the supply chain and in the store[5]; and

- GPS-based mobile apps allow researchers to contact people at different points on their customer journey.

IDEO, a global consulting firm, has become very successful at applying "design thinking" and facilitating the creative participation of customers to design innovative services. Today, it helps organizations design products, services, environments, and digital experiences.

A second major concern is that the "gates" which often rely on traditional business or financial criteria to screen ideas may screen out new services at too early a stage. A solution is to conduct innovation in a separate organizational unit. Ideas must be nurtured and fleshed out in an organizational unit that has an in-depth understanding of the customer before external financial criteria are imposed.

Case Study: M-PESA in Kenya

Vodafone and Safaricom partnered to develop a mobile banking service called M-PESA, which enables Kenyans to transfer money via short message service (SMS). Customers buy digital funds from local shops that act as M-PESA agents. They can then electronically transfer these funds to any other mobile phone user. M-PESA is extremely popular with Kenyans because many do not have bank accounts, yet they need to send or receive small amounts of cash. M-PESA charges very modest fees to send or receive cash. Vodafone currently intends to introduce this service in international markets. However, at its early stages, M-PESA might not have surmounted Vodafone's financial hurdles. It benefited from development within Safaricom by managers who saw how Kenyans used SMS in innovative ways.

Third, many organizations seek ways to increase the *speed* of innovation. Chinese organizations are accelerating innovation by creating separate teams to work simultaneously on different stages of the new product development process, coordinated by a leader.[6] Many firms, such as Tencent QQ, launch new services at a very early stage and then solicit customer feedback to improve them. Tencent QQ offers a variety of services, including online social games, music, shopping, microblogging, movies, platform of games, and group and voice chat. How does it achieve customer participation in the innovation process? It has created channels to encourage rapid customer feedback and rapidly communicate it to the R&D team, thereby ensuring that the design process is sufficiently flexible to incorporate new functionality quickly into the customer experience.

Positioning Offerings Along the Service Infusion Continuum

Services are an attractive path to organic growth. Organizations often obtain higher margins from services.[7] Hence, a common way for managers to think about service innovation is from a positioning perspective. Specifically, they imagine a service infusion continuum anchored by goods-centric offerings at one end, such as warranties or maintenance services, and customer-focused services at the other end, such as business solution services.[8] From this standpoint, the organization has the opportunity to develop new service offerings at any point on this continuum and the key managerial question becomes: Where to position along the service infusion continuum?

Some experts argue that a single organization can design and deliver offerings at multiple points along the continuum.[9] In a study of Swedish firms, they observed organizations making both evolutionary and revolutionary changes in service content—with firms infusing additional services and phasing out services. Most organizations seemed to make evolutionary progress—slowly introducing services initiated by customer demand. However, some organizations achieved revolutionary changes by working hard to build strong relations with their customers and then introducing new services that transform how the two parties collaborate. For example, Volvo Aero introduced its "power by the hour" concept (inspired by General Electric), which only charges customers for the time an airplane engine is used.

Two critical factors influencing the success of service infusion are:

- The organization's capability to deliver the new service offering; and

- The risks arising from customer acceptance, participation, and willingness to pay.

For example, GE Healthcare has partnered with Temple University Health System to design imaging services that are effective from a diagnostic standpoint, but also cost-effective to deliver in developing countries. This partnership increases their joint capabilities and decreases the risk of market failure. Interestingly, organizations can simultaneously offer similar services at different points on the continuum.[10] Another example is that a customer can pick up a rental car after using self-service technology or the rental car company can bring the car to the customer. The two experiences are completely different. The organizational capabilities required for each service experience—as well as the nature of customer participation—are quite different from each other, too.

This chapter now considers four organizational tools for service innovation. They are:

1. The *Gap Model* provides a framework for designing and delivering excellent service experiences for customers;
2. *Service Blueprinting* develops a diagnostic flowchart of the customer experience;
3. The *Critical Incident Technique* (*CIT*) and *Root Cause Analysis*, both provide a mechanism for sustaining and improving customer experiences; and
4. *Benchmarking* helps organization learn by studying best-in-class or best-in-world processes.

Identifying Gaps in Creating an Excellent Service Experience

Organizations may fail to design and deliver service that meets customer needs because they do not follow fundamental marketing principles: segmenting markets according to customer needs and designing services that build relational bonds with customers. A strategic approach for designing new service experiences (or improving existing service experiences) for customers that has been used by many organizations is the *Gap Model*.[11] It focuses on systematically reducing the difference between customers' perceptions and their expectations regarding the customer experience. The "Customer Gap" is the primary gap. It is the discrepancy between customer's needs and expectations and the current customer experience (as it is delivered by the organization). It is created by Gaps 1 to 4, as depicted in Figure 6.1.

Gap 1, the "Listening Gap," arises from not knowing what customers expect due to insufficient information about customers. It can be remedied through better utilization of marketing research, business analytics, increased interactions between management and customers, and better communication between managers and customer contact employees. A major challenge is that there are many new ways to listen to (and observe) customers—and that diverse sources of data (such as clickstream, eye-tracking, and RFID data) must be integrated and analyzed to generate useable insights. Organizations must develop new capabilities—often involving

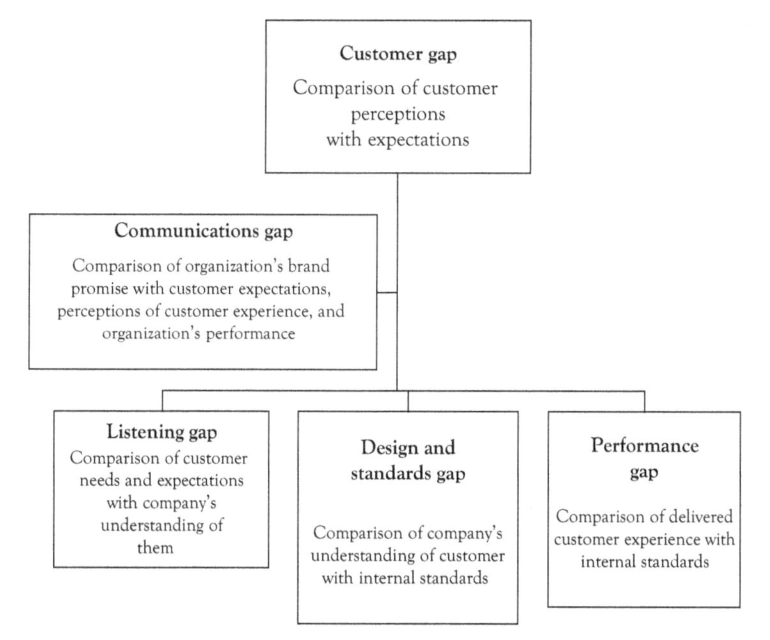

Figure 6.1 The Gap Model

Source: Adapted from Parasuraman, Zeithaml, and Berry (1985a).

real-time assimilation of customer information—and new processes to translate information into better service for customers. For example, by tracking the paths of supermarket shopping carts, one study discovered that the presence of other shoppers attracts consumers toward a store zone but reduces consumers' tendency to shop there.[12] At the same time, most organizations still need traditional methods of directly listening to the customer, such as focus groups, in-depth interviews, ethnographic techniques, and surveys.

Gap 2, the "Design and Standards Gap," arises from not having service designs and standards that reflect customers' expectations. It can be remedied by creating a formal process for setting goals for the customer experience and then standardizing policies and procedures for employees and operations. A major challenge is bringing together managers from different functional areas and aligning their goals based on customer needs and goals.

Gap 3, the "Service Performance Gap," arises when execution of the service fails to meet its internal service standards. Service performance is the responsibility of people, including employees, network partners, and (sometimes) customers. Employee contributions to the service experience can be improved by refining recruitment strategies for employees, improving training for employees so that they understand how to perform their roles, ensuring that organizational goals are not in conflict, supporting employees with technology and tools, and aligning evaluation, compensation, and rewards for employees to match service performance goals. Network partners' contributions to service experiences can be improved by aligning interorganizational goals, creating performance metrics that are consistent with goals, linking rewards and costs to the achievement of goals, controlling consistency across channels. Chapter 8 discusses these issues.

Gap 4, the "Communication Gap," arises when the service experience doesn't match the organization's promises to customers. This gap can be remedied by improving external communications with customers, such as eliminating overpromising in advertising, personal selling, or other situations in which the organization influences customer expectations. Physical evidence also communicates information about the customer experience, so it may be necessary to consider the role of service personnel uniforms, site décor, and so on. Price also acts as a quality signal, so the organization may need to re-evaluate the value proposition. The communication gap can also be remedied by better internal communication and management of service promises, such as service guarantees, policies, and procedures that are utilized across organizational units. Chapter 8 discusses physical evidence, communication, and branding further.

Point to Ponder: Apply the *Gap Model* to an organization with which you are familiar. What insights does this analysis generate?

Service Blueprinting

A well-established tool for designing new service processes or improving existing service processes is the service blueprint. It has been used successfully by many member companies of the Center for Services Leadership at Arizona State University. A service blueprint is a map of activities that are involved in the coproduction or cocreation of service.[13] It is sometimes called process mapping or activity mapping. It is analogous to flowcharting by industrial engineers, except that the focus is on the mapping of service processes, rather than activities associated with a unit of output. A typical service blueprint distinguishes between four types of service processes:[14]

- Customer actions
- Onstage contact employee actions
- Backstage contact employee actions
- Support processes

A service blueprint brings together people, processes, and tangibles in an integrative fashion. The map typically uses the horizontal axis to represent time and the vertical axis to model the component and subcomponent processes. Enterprise Rent-A-Car Company, the leading rental car company in the United States, locates its offices close to where people live and work, and offers customer pickup and drop-off service. The novelty of Enterprise's decentralized service system is quickly apparent when its service blueprint is compared with the service blueprint for (say) the Hertz Corp which targets travelers and locates outlets at airports or other central locations.

There are many reasons why organizations find service blueprints to be useful in identifying new service opportunities.

- The map focuses on the customer's role in the service process.
- A new process can be designed—or an existing process can be examined and improved—by viewing it as an interconnected whole, so that opportunities and challenges can be anticipated or isolated. For example, a blueprint is very useful for understanding time and cost trade-offs for both the customer and the organization.
- A service blueprint can help identify customer–employee interaction points, bottlenecks, and the locus of service failures.
- By comparing service blueprints for the same process in different organizational units, blueprinting can help establish standard operating procedures based on best practices.
- Blueprints can be the basis for setting goals for employees, for integration of cross-functional processes, and for internal and external quality management.

Point to Ponder: Blueprint a simple service operation where you have access to backstage processes. How does the map help identify ways to improve service?

Critical Incidents and Root Cause Analysis

Critical incidents are especially satisfying or dissatisfying service experiences. Organizations find it useful to study critical incidents to understand the factors that influence perceptions of their experiences at a design and process level (rather than an overall relationship level). The CIT is a way of studying service experiences to identify the factors that lead to occasions when customers are either very disappointed or highly delighted.[15] Organizations survey customers and ask them to report (in their own words) about critical incidents, with questions such as:

Think of a time when, as a customer, you had a particularly satisfying (dissatisfying) interaction with an employee. When did the incident happen? What specific circumstances led up to this situation? Exactly what did the service provider say or do? What made you feel the interaction was satisfying (dissatisfying)?

The goal is to identify and correct deficiencies in service, as well as identify ways of providing superior service. The CIT is especially helpful in identifying where service processes break down or are in conflict.

***Point to Ponder*:** Describe a critical incident in which an organization failed to meet (or exceeded) your expectations. How did you react? Would you use this organization again?

Service failures are especially pivotal moments for customers, many of whom experience strong emotional reactions to a service failure and to the organization's service recovery efforts—that is, the organization's actions in response to a service failure. For example, in 2015, German carmaker Volkswagen recalled diesel engine vehicles after admitting to having manipulated emissions testing data in Europe. Customers are more emotionally involved in and more observant of organizations' attempts to "recover" from service failures than they are of routine or first-time service. In fact, customers are often more dissatisfied by an organization's failure to recover than by the service failure itself.[16] This observation is equally true in B2B experiences in which reliable and responsive service from suppliers is critical to the buying organization's business success. For this reason, organizations should encourage complaints about poor service and be highly attentive in remedying them. Chapter 7 addresses how to respond to service failures.[17]

Root cause analyses can originate from an analysis of internal metrics. For example, suppose a company has tracked social media reports complaining that service is unreliable—some customers are waiting a long time for a response to a service request. The company might then undertake a root cause analysis using internal records. It might generate a histogram or frequency distribution describing how long it takes to complete a service request or to identify specific requests that had very long elapsed times, and look for root causes. The goal is to identify ways that underlying processes that could be made more effective and efficient. By improving the underlying process, the organization can improve the consistency of the customer experience.

For example, Panera Bread Company realized that it wasn't leveraging its customer survey information sufficiently. To understand the customer experience, it needed to tie survey responses to in-store customer experiences. It randomly e-mailed customers who had visited their café. An analysis of survey responses from those customers who had used Panera's rapid pickup service discovered that some orders were inaccurate and recovery after these inaccurate orders were associated with a lack of team warmth. Panera managers' root cause analyses led them to introduce a service guarantee that the café would fix the error right away and give the customer a free treat. The guarantee communicated to customers and employees the importance of the customer experience.

Case Study: Innovation at MSA Safety Incorporated

MSA Safety is a global maker of sophisticated safety products that help protect workers who may be exposed to a variety of hazardous conditions. MSA Asia Pacific created a small customer experience (CX) team, composed of managers representing different functional areas. They were tasked with improving the customer experience and tracking the impact on revenues. The CX team began by blueprinting six major underlying processes that provide the foundation for the customer experience. For MSA, they were: the customer conducts research and makes a decision regarding a supplier, she selects a configuration of products and makes a purchase, delivery and installation occurs, a service team provides ongoing support, and (ultimately) the customer evaluates the partnership experience. The CX team held sessions with different employee groups to identify bottlenecks and sources of failure. About 150 items were identified and grouped into clusters based on their root causes. Employees were asked to prioritize these items—identifying 10 high priority items.

The CX team then invited its channel partners and (separately) customers from a few major accounts to a special three hour meeting. Participants were invited to describe their perceptions of each of the six major processes, as well as their needs and expectations for each process. The MSA hosts focused on listening and probing to obtain a deep understanding of the customer experience. Each meeting concluded with participants identifying high priority items that they considered critical incidents or moments of truth. Later, the CX team compared employee and customer priorities and discovered there was considerable overlap in the two groups of items. However, in two areas, customers gave high priority to items that employees didn't consider important. This observation was a wake-up call. The CX team worked systematically to improve the high priority items—with special emphasis on the customer experience for its largest customers (who were likely to be its most valuable). In several cases, small changes in MSA service processes substantially improved the customer experience. Customer feedback was overwhelmingly positive. After a year, MSA Asia Pacific gross profits were 20 percent higher—at a time when its competitors' revenues were shrinking.

Benchmarking

Some organizations, such as Dell, are fanatical about benchmarking. Their rationale is that it always makes sense to learn new ways to design and deliver service from best practices in other industries. Moreover, managers are often motivated to improve when they compare the organization's service processes with others' processes. This comparison is called benchmarking. They should start by identifying a particular process that needs improvement (based on customer priorities) and then identify organizations outside their industry that excel at this process. Since pricing and new product development processes tend to be highly confidential, managers should focus on business processes, human resource processes, and customer satisfaction efforts.

For example, suppose that the process needing improvement is training customer service representatives. After identifying the information that is needed, the manager can reach out to a cooperating organization and arrange a visit to collect the information. The visit should be made by a small group of process owners, in this case, the employees that train customer service representatives. The group should be prepared to share information about how they manage the training process. Any shared information by either party should be treated as confidential and not shared with other companies. By comparing the organization with the benchmark organization, the team can identify performance gaps. Ways to improve the gaps can be identified by sharing the findings internally and developing goals and an action plan. Once the action plan is implemented, it should be monitored and adjusted as needed.

Another form of benchmarking compares customer survey ratings of the service experience with similar ratings from competitors' customers. Ratings of different aspects of the customer experience can be compared to identify strengths and weaknesses.

This chapter concludes by describing four tools for identifying improvements in the customer experience: KPI's, business analytics, surveys and dashboards.

Key Process Indicators: Hard and Soft Measures

KPIs are a useful source of information about how to innovate or improve business models, processes, or products. An organization's service standards should be based on the customer experience; it should be possible for managers to take actions to improve them, and they should be achievable given the service operations environment.[18] Companies usually use a combination of hard standards—that is, engineering and operations metrics—and external standards derived from customers—that is, surveys, social media, or purchase behavior. External standards become actionable for managers if they are linked to objective and concrete service standards that can be monitored and managed. There will be different service standards for different process within different organizational units, depending on their purpose.

Many organizations focus on KPIs that reflect service performance levels, such as on-time delivery times, that have a major effect on the customer experience. The targets for the KPIs are service design standards that should be aligned with customer expectations. Many organizations have been able to substantially improve the customer experience by

Case Study: Improving the Customer Experience at Best Western Hotels

Best Western International operates more than 4,000 hotels—more than half in the United States. It tracks operational metrics that tie directly to the customer experience for each property, plus comments by customers from social media. Every hotel manager can access this information via a web portal and, at some properties, other employees who work on the property can also see it. By providing employees with metrics for a specific property, the system makes employees accountable for the customer experience. An interesting feature of this approach is that employees receive feedback directly from customers, rather than from their supervisors, which makes training and coaching much easier.

monitoring KPIs and finding ways to innovate or improve underlying service processes.

How are customer-driven standards developed?

1. Track customer satisfaction versus internal measures of key processes (e.g., response times).
2. Build predictive models or use statistical analyses to uncover more complex drivers of customer perceptions.

Tracking

Some fairly simple analyses can help managers identify appropriate customer-based service standards. For example, Figure 6.2 shows customer satisfaction ratings (a soft standard) plotted on a graph against the amount of time that elapsed before a customer's service request was acted upon (a hard standard). There is a steep drop in satisfaction ratings for large business customers after a four hour delay, whereas satisfaction ratings for small business customers fall less rapidly. The graph shows that large customers have different standards than small customers, suggesting that the firm should consider offering same-day service to large business customers and next-day service to small business customers. In this particular case, the firm learned that small business customers preferred a specific appointment time for a service call (rather than rush service)

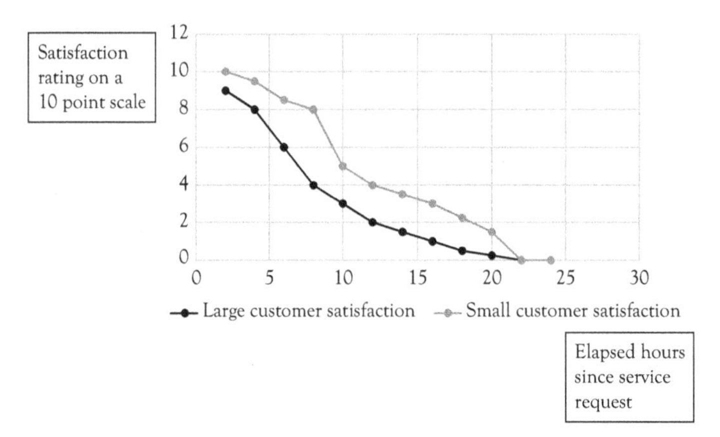

Figure 6.2 The relationship between customer satisfaction and speed of response

because it was hard for them to handle unexpected interruptions during the business day.

Many studies have shown that a customer's ratings of a service experience—and her repurchase behavior—can be directly linked to engineering and operations measures. A telecommunications company replaced local telephone cables and tracked a fall in consumer ratings in the short run, followed by a rise in ratings six months later.[19] A computing systems support supplier found that business customer's likelihood of renewing a service contract depended on engineer work minutes previously allocated to the contract, as well as engineer work minutes allocated to other contracts from the same supplier.[20] Engineering and operations measures describing the customer experience have also been linked to customers' willingness to pay for service.[21]

Modeling

Statistical analyses or predictive models based on measures of the customer experience can uncover important customer insights. For example, a system support supplier was interested in identifying hard or soft standards related to the customer's perception of "prompt service." Managers conducted statistical analyses and identified two operations metrics that were tied to customers' survey ratings for responsiveness: (1) the time, measured in minutes, between when an initial service request was made and the representative acted on the request and (2) the supervisor's evaluation of the customer service representative's handling of request. (Supervisors routinely rated each representative monthly by listening to calls.) The organization chose these two metrics as internal service quality standards—and established targets for each. Managers were able to improve the organization's speed of response by changing staffing schedules to handle peak periods of service requests, without any decrease in supervisors' ratings of call handling. In this way, the organization was able to improve responsiveness and consequently the entire customer experience.

Business Analytics

As the analysis of big data has become more tractable, organizations have used business analytics to learn about the customer experience and the customer journey. In this way, organizations can leverage data to align service strategies and tactics with customer needs. In addition, managers can identify significant customer events—such as service failures—without the inevitable time lapse that occurs with many traditional market research methods. Equally importantly, business analytics may be able to *predict* when these events will occur for customers—so that the organization can make adjustments to its processes and deliver an excellent service experience. Many business processes generate data that can be leveraged in these three ways. Hence, the big data explosion enhances and complements traditional methods of listening to customers.

Case Study: Dell Global Sales Improves Its Fulfillment Processes

Dell Inc. knows from listening to customers that an excellent customer experience requires on-time fulfillment of customer orders. For this reason, Dell Global Sales Operations monitors 12 KPIs for fulfillment in real time. It built predictive models of how orders move through the fulfillment system. Using the model, it was able to identify gaps in its fulfillment process—in real time—and intervene to improve the timeliness of shipments to customers. The result was a 54 percent increase in on-time deliveries. The use of business analytics accelerated the company's actions—better aligning it with customer needs.

How did Dell achieve its success? Interestingly, the company's key challenge was *not* the development of its predictive models. Rather, its key challenge was using the information provided by the business analytics to take actions that improved the customer experience. Dell created customer experience champions within the company. The champions led efforts to change business processes within the company. They harnessed the efforts of existing functional groups with the company. Action plans were developed through an iterative process of trial and improvement. Next, Dell documented successful efforts and developed a training program so that key learnings could be disseminated across the entire organization. They also recognized customer experience champions in a "Hall of Fame" on their website.

A key step is unifying different sources of data so that service operations metrics are linked to information about customer satisfaction with the service experience, spending and share of wallet. The integration of internal and external data allows managers to identify ways to improve marketing effectiveness, achieve targeted service levels, and identify opportunities for market expansion. It also allows the organization to be more agile in responding to customers and the marketplace. Many managers agree that the key challenge is deciding which data to analyze—and ensuring that the appropriate capabilities are available to apply key learnings to improve the customer experience. In particular, sales and service teams must learn to leverage the new insights that are being generated.

Business analytics also provide opportunities to identify new sources of revenues from customers that create topline growth. B2B organizations have been especially successful at increasing revenues from customers by improving the service experience. At Intel, business analytics uncovered the startling fact that retailer inventory levels were low—often only 65 percent of products were available on the shelf at any given time. Intel was able to use business analytics to substantially increase product on-shelf availability, thereby increasing sales revenue substantially.

Managers frequently discover that "big data" is not the same as "deep data." Inevitably, it will be necessary to take a deep dive into the customer experience. Customer data—including ethnographic data and netnographic data—are helpful in interpreting business analytics or suggesting managerial questions that can be investigated with business analytics. The reason for this approach is that business analytics don't generate key insights—but they do enable them to be tested. Tracking customer comments about the service brand on social media allow organizations to monitor customer experiences in real time and identify trends at an early stage. For example, a customer suggested that a Personal Beauty Advisor could help Sephora customers select products. Sephora was able to test this idea in some stores and then evaluate its effectiveness using business analytics. Qualitative studies are also useful in developing powerful stories that convey the customer experience to people within the organization who must create and deliver the service experience.

***Point to Ponder*:** How does your organization use cross-functional teams when developing new services or making service improvements? Are "behind the scenes" operations aligned with customers' expectations about the service experience?

Common Survey Measures

Since service is intangible and the customer experience is created during production and consumption, organizations require a survey program that tracks customer perceptions of their experiences. Organizations use many different measures of customers' perceptions. Usually, these measures are elicited by surveys that are administered online or by telephone. For example, service quality ratings are typically used to compare organizational units that deliver the same service (e.g., comparing customer service centers or repair depots). Surveys are most useful when they are tied directly to a specific customer experience or to internal operations metrics that describe the experience—it is the integration of these measures that makes them actionable for organizations. Hence, managers may analyze survey data in conjunction with engineering or operations measures to obtain diagnostic measures of the performance of specific service processes (such as accurate and on-time delivery). Since managers require measures for many different purposes, there are many different survey measures in use within most organizations.

The most commonly used survey questions elicit ratings of:

1. Perceived service quality and value;
2. Customer satisfaction; and
3. Intentions to repurchase or recommend (also called loyalty).

In most developed countries, there are well-established survey programs that track service quality and satisfaction in specific industries. In the United States, the three best-known surveys are SERVQUAL, the American Customer Satisfaction Index (ACSI), and Net Promoter Score. The SERVQUAL questionnaire measures *perceived* service quality, defined as a customer's evaluation of the overall excellence or superiority of the service,[22] and evaluates its five underlying dimensions.[23] The ACSI reports customer satisfaction scores on a 0 to 100 scale at the national level.[24] Although participation in the ACSI is optional, it has been widely accepted by industry and government. The Net Promoter Score measures purchase and recommendation intentions. The particular metric used by an organization usually depends on the industry in which they compete and the goals they are pursuing. There are many different industry-specific surveys, such as the J.D. Powers Guest Satisfaction Index in the hotel industry. The next three sections briefly describe some metrics, the purposes for which they are designed, their advantages, and disadvantages.

Service Quality and Value

Service quality is a customers' judgment about the excellence or superiority of a service.[25] Customers may rely on intrinsic and extrinsic attributes, such as price, brand name, advertising, and corporate reputation, in evaluating quality.[26] Since they may choose to rely on extrinsic attributes, customers are usually willing to make a quality judgment of a service even when they have not used it (based on what they know). Perceived service quality is often measured on a scale from poor to excellent—although other rating scales may be preferable for statistical reasons. This measure is helpful when managers wish to monitor or track on service quality—and they do not intend to link it to repurchase intentions, loyalty, or word-of-mouth. For example, measures of service quality can be useful when a manager's goal is to study a specific service process, such as repair, installation, or billing, as well as the overall service experience. However, it is important to remember that customers usually don't consider price or price fairness when they answer questions about service quality—and they may consider extrinsic attributes, such as advertising, that weren't part of the experience. Hence, the relationship between measures of service quality and customer purchase behavior may be difficult to detect without advanced statistical models.

Organizations are also very interested in understanding how a customer evaluates their service experiences or relationships. Unfortunately, customers tend to assign many different means to the word "value," which makes survey questions about value extremely problematic. For customers, good value can mean "low price," "what I want," "the quality I get for the price I pay," or "what I get for what I give."[27] Hence, survey ratings of value are difficult for managers to interpret. In general, customers' perceptions of value depend on their perceptions of quality, price, nonmonetary costs, and extrinsic attributes. They do not depend on emotions. Organizations sometimes elicit survey ratings about value as part of a battery of survey measures—usually when they are trying to understand how customers are responding to price.

Customer Satisfaction

Scholarly research has repeatedly shown that individual customers' satisfaction with their service experience increases customer retention, purchases or usage, and cross-buying—as well as decreasing customer complaints and the likelihood of customer defection.[28] Consequently, the organization benefits from increased revenues that arise from existing customers' increased purchases, willingness to pay a price premium, and positive word of mouth,[29] as well as the organization's improved ability to attract new customers. The organization also benefits from decreased costs to serve customers because the organization and the customer interact more effectively and efficiently.

Customers' satisfaction with their experiences is associated with business success at the firm level, as well as the level of the individual customer.[30] Many studies have used data from an independent national survey, such as the ACSI, that obtains customer satisfaction ratings for firms in all sectors of the national economy. (Similar data exists in other countries.) There is some evidence that the ACSI index is a leading indicator of stock prices.[31] Organizations with customers who are very satisfied with their experience tend to have higher and more stable net cash flows—suggesting that investments in improving the customer experience are high return and low risk.[32] A third study investigated the trade-off between investments in labor versus automation (self-service) in the United States; it concluded that investments in technology can increase service productivity, customer satisfaction, and profitability. However, for high price, high margin services, investments in labor can be warranted to ensure high quality customer experience and satisfaction.

In general, high satisfaction with the customer experience is associated with high customer retention rates. (It usually requires sophisticated statistical models to show the nature of the relationship.) However, there are certain exceptions. Customers may become "trapped" in the short run—perhaps due to switching costs—so that they are unhappy but appear to be loyal. In the long run, they will find ways to "vote with their feet." For example, in many countries, government-run post offices traditionally handled most mail and parcel delivery services. However, when alternative service providers become available, customers defect to obtain more customized service, such as same-day delivery. In addition, there are other factors—beyond customer satisfaction that enhance the customer experience and increase retention. For example, as discussed in Chapter 4, customers are likely to evaluate the organization's reputation, its relevance to the customers' future needs, and the fairness of its prices vis-à-vis competitors when they decide whether to repurchase.

Intentions to Purchase and Recommend to Others

Many organizations measure customers' intentions to purchase or recommend the brand. For example, Net Promoter Score™ has become very popular. Some managers believe that a combination of higher repeat purchase intentions and willingness to recommend indicates that customers will be ambassadors or advocates for the organization. An example of a purchase intentions question is: "I am thinking of using organization XXX for my next online purchase," where the scale is anchored with 1 = completely disagree and 5 = completely agree. The underlying rationale is that these measures are often considered to reflect customers' loyalty—where loyalty is defined as an underlying predisposition or deeply held commitment to repurchase a preferred product or service consistently in the future.[33] However, the intentions-behavior linkage holds in some industries but not in others. In general, self-reported intentions can only serve as proxies for future behavior. Many academic studies have shown that intentions are not good predictors of purchase behavior and that the underlying determinants of intentions and behavior are quite different.[34] In particular, purchase intentions will not be good predictors of future behavior when the context of the customer experience changes—due to changes in their preferences, competition, or the marketplace. Changes will inevitably happen in the long term, if not in the short term.

Dashboards and Multiple Metrics

Many managers will ask: "What is the single best measure to track over time?" Unfortunately, there is no "one size fits all" method for measuring and managing the customer experience. The reason is that customers will weigh different experiential attributes and different customer experience building blocks differently in each industry. Moreover, different external (survey) and internal measures are used for different managerial purposes. For example, a sensitive measure is typically used to detect the effects of specific service changes whereas a relatively stable measure is preferable when survey measures are linked to employee or team incentives. An example of a sensitive measure is: "On a five point scale, how would you rate your online shopping experience with Firm XXX: better ... the same or ... worse than expected?" A more stable measure might be: "How satisfied are you with your online shopping experience with Firm XXX? where 1 = not very satisfied and 5 = very satisfied."

As we emphasized in Chapter 4, there are many ingredients of the customer experience that organizations may track, such as emotional responses or price fairness. In summary, there will always be a need for a variety of metrics, as well as market research studies, to obtain a

Table 6.1 Improving the customer experience: goals, metrics, and methods

Think about the customer experience with respect to a specific process, program, or product. Identify the process, program, or product here for which you are identifying customer experience goals.		
Objectives or goals (e.g., product, process, or program that is measured)	**Types of measures** (e.g., overall or transaction satisfaction, attribute performance, complaints)	**Measurement methods** (e.g., qualitative versus quantitative, type [internal, survey, etc.], timing and frequency, reporting method)
Component # 1:		
Component # 2:		
Component # 3:		

comprehensive view of the customer experience. Many organizations provide managers with dashboards or other decision-making tools that provide views of key performance indicators relevant to a particular function or process. Managers can use a dashboard that shows multiple metrics in the same way a driver uses the dashboard in a car. Specifically, the dashboard provides a manager with summary information, key trends (upward or down), comparisons with targets and so on.

Regardless of where it starts, every organization needs to improve the customer experience and build stronger relationships that create value for the organization. The best way to get started is to take one step—make incremental improvements and learn as you improve. For example, a first step might be to use Table 6.1 to help clarify your thoughts about the customer experience, how it is measured and how it is managed.

As you look at Table 6.1, ask yourself the following questions.

1. What processes have the largest impact on the customer experience and are the greatest source of revenues?
2. Identify three customer experience goals *for a specific process, program, or product* in your organization. Write them in the left column.

   a. How familiar are managers in your company with the steps involved in carrying out the process?
   b. The customer experience building blocks shown in Figure 4.1 provide a useful list of factors important to the holistic customer experience. Do these goals capture the important features of the customer experience?
3. Describe the measures your organization uses to evaluate its performance for each goal. Write them in the middle column and add any descriptive information about the measurement method in the right column.
   a. Are these measures customer-driven standards?
   b. Are they hard standards or soft standards?
   c. How timely are the measures?
4. What is your assessment of how measures are tracked and compared to goals? Is there a feedback loop for improvement?
   a. Are there any key aspects of the customer experience (related to these three goals) that are not measured?
   b. If your organization has many measures, is there a clear linkage between these measures and organizational goals? Are organizational priorities clear?
5. After reflecting on Question 4, select three aspects of the customer experience that aren't measured (and should be) or three "disconnects" in how measures link to goals.
   a. If information is missing, what kinds of research efforts could you undertake to ensure that your worksheet is as comprehensive as possible?
   b. How can these challenges in Question 4 can be mapped into organizational programs or tasks.
   c. How familiar are managers in your organization with your organization's customer experience goals, how they are measured and tracked, and what measures are needed to make improvements?
6. If your organization lacks knowledge or capabilities in this area, consider benchmarking.
   a. What companies meet the highest standards in performing these core processes?

b. How would you choose representatives to serve on a benchmarking team?
c. What could your company do to train the team members?
d. What problems might crop up at the implementation stage?

If you don't know the answers to some of these questions, think about how you will obtain this information. Begin with small steps. Eventually, your organization may need a dashboard or business analytics tool that enables them to monitor different aspects of the customer experience and take action to improve the customer experience. However, the best way to get started is to pick a specific project.

Point to Ponder: Many organizations talk about delivering an excellent customer experience. However, few actually devote significant time, effort, and resources to designing, delivering, and evaluating the quality of the service experience from the customer's viewpoint. What are some of the ways that successful companies have improved the customer experience? What metrics are needed to help managers make decisions?

Key Ideas

- Innovation in the modern marketplace frequently leverages networks of organizations, connected in novel ways through technology. Hence, an organization may wish to partner with others to increase its capability to successfully introduce a new offering and reduce the risks that customers won't be willing to buy it.
- Customer-focused innovation requires that the stage-gate process should be different than the process for manufactured goods:
  - Customers should participate in early and late stages of the development process.
  - Innovations should be nurtured so that the organization can't impose inappropriate financial hurdles that can shut down innovation.

  - Fast, iterative testing of service concepts helps bring offerings to market.
  - Customers don't make decisions about new product development and innovation. They provide information that helps managers make decisions.
- The implementation of a service-centered strategy requires a well-designed and executed customer experience that exceeds expectations, plus the development of service recovery procedures that anticipate potential failures.
- Consider innovation frameworks, such as the service infusion continuum, the *Gaps Model, Service Blueprinting,* the *CIT, Root Cause Analysis,* and *Benchmarking,* to create excellent customer experiences.
- Discover different ways to improve the customer experience, by using *KPIs, Business Analytics, Metrics* (both *Internal Standards* and external *Survey-based measures*) and *Dashboards* for monitoring and managing a 360° view of the customer experience over time.

Notes

1. Urban and Hauser (1993).
2. Chang and Taylor (2016).
3. Shankar, Berry, and Dotzel (2009).
4. Functional magnetic resonance imaging (FMRI) displays images that can show an increase in blood flow in the brain, a result of churning neurons that are demanding extra oxygen. See: Chase (2006) for a layman's description of it and other techniques.
5. Hui, Bradlow, and Fader (2009).
6. Williamson and Yin (2014).
7. Reichheld and Teal (2001).
8. Zeithaml et al. (2015).
9. Fundin, Wittel, and Gebauer (2012).
10. Campbell, Maglio, and Davis (2011).
11. Parasuraman, Zeithaml, and Berry (1985b); Zeithaml, Parasuraman, and Berry (1990).

12. Hui, Bradlow, and Fader (2009).
13. Shostack (1984).
14. Zeithaml and Bitner (2000).
15. Bitner, Booms, and Tetreault (1990).
16. Bitner, Booms, and Tetreault (1990); Smith and Bolton (1998).
17. Government regulations may require companies to disclosure certain types of information, reply to complaints within set time limits, and publish written procedures for handling customer satisfaction.
18. Bolton and Drew (1994).
19. Bolton and Drew (1994).
20. Bolton, Lemon, and Bramlett (2006).
21. Bolton and Myers (2003).
22. Zeithaml (1988); Quality has been defined in a variety of ways, including conformance to specifications, conformance to requirements, and fitness for use. From our perspective, the key point is that quality must be defined from the customers' perspective—not the organizations' perspective—and must encompass all benefits generated by the value creation process.
23. Parasuraman, Zeithaml, and Berry (1988).
24. Fornell et al. (1996).
25. Zeithaml (1988).
26. Bolton and Drew (1991a, 1991b).
27. Zeithaml (1988).
28. Bolton (1998); Bolton and Lemon (1999); Bolton, Lemon, and Bramlett (2006); Cooil et al. (2007); Crosby and Stephens (1987); Kamakura et al. (2003); Verhoef (2003).
29. Anderson (1998); Anderson and Sullivan (1993).
30. Anderson, Fornell, and Lehmann (1994); Anderson, Fornell, and Rust (1997); Rust and Zahorik (1993).
31. Anderson and Fornell (2000).
32. Fornell et al. (2006).
33. Oliver (1999).
34. Morwitz and Schmittlein (1992); Seiders et al. (2005).

CHAPTER 7

Service Design and Multichannel Management

A service-centered perspective requires organizations to manage and coordinate a larger set of functions. For goods, managers typically make decisions about:

- **P**rice;
- **P**roduct;
- **P**romotion; and
- **P**lace (i.e., distribution or supply chains and networks).

However, service-centric organizations that focus on the customer experience manage and coordinate additional decisions concerning:[1]

- **P**rocesses;
- **P**eople; and
- **P**hysical evidence.

Processes, people, and physical evidence are critical to the creation and delivery of the customer experience. Hence, Chapters 7 and 8 discuss these last three activities, beginning with designing and managing processes.

Process refers to the procedures and activities through which service is cocreated and delivered to customers. In many organizations, service processes are referred to as service operations or standard procedures. Service processes can be very complex, such as an airline company's or hospital's operations—or relatively simple, such as hair styling. This chapter focuses on four key issues concerning business processes which influence the customer experience:

1. Service design
2. Multichannel management
3. How customer experiences differ (or not) across channels
4. How channels create value for organizations

In addition, no matter how well an organization designs its business processes and channels, every organization will occasionally fail to deliver an excellent customer experience. Hence, this chapter also discusses:

5. Service failure and recovery strategies.

Service Design

Customers prefer well-designed service experiences. People respond to good design in art, fashion, and architecture, but sometimes managers overlook this important observation in designing the customer experience.[2] Good design doesn't just mean "eye-pleasing." What does it mean to cocreate well-designed experiences with customers?

- Customers appreciate good design because human beings prefer integrity, completeness, and wholeness. So, for example, a customer experience must be delivered in a seamless fashion—where technology and employees behave synergistically, as opposed to making conflicting demands on customers. Also, customers need closure on a service recovery process—not being "left hanging."
- Customers appreciate good design because people have an innate preference for symmetry and balance—and feel uncomfortable when elements of the customer experience seem incongruous and don't fit with the brand. So, for example, a retail store must support the employees and customer experiences that take place within it, not simply appeal to a specific aesthetic taste (see Chapter 8). Also, as emphasized elsewhere, customers' perceptions of fairness or "balance" in how people, both employees and customers, are treated is important in the customer experience.

Case Study: IBM Adopts Design Thinking to Grow Revenues

IBM is reinventing itself by adopting design thinking as a way to grow revenues.[3] Like many established companies, IBM's goal is to grow its new businesses faster than its older, lucrative businesses decline. According to Phil Gilbert, General Manager of Design, the key to design thinking is to identify users' needs as a starting point, not come up with product ideas and then try to sell them. IBM is hiring 1,000 professional designers and training its workforce of 370,000 employees in design thinking. They are being embedded in product teams to work alongside customers or to work in one of 24 design studios around the world. IBM has also invested heavily in new fields such as data analytics and cloud computing. However, design thinking is required to put the customer experience at the center of IBM's new business growth activities. Customers often collaborate with IBM developers to write cloud software applications, such as Bluemix, a software platform that has attracted many developers. The infusion of design strategy will create a more diversified customer mix.

Although services dominate economic activity in developed economies, innovation in services is extremely challenging for three reasons.

1. The customer experience is cocreated with customers—implying that a new service must be designed with intimate knowledge of how customers interact with the organization's people, processes, and tangibles to produce mutually beneficial outcomes.
2. Investment in research and development regarding services lags behind similar investments for manufactured goods.
3. Very little is known about new service *design*.

Some experts argue that service design should begin with the new service concept,[4] which is a detailed description of the customer needs to be satisfied, how they are to be satisfied, what is to be done for the customer, and how this is to be achieved. Note that this kind of design thinking maps very directly onto the customer experience.

Many managers find it useful to think about service processes using a theater metaphor so they can distinguish between backstage processes—that take place where the customer can't observe them—or front-stage processes—that the customer observes and possibly participates.[5] An example is provided by an insurance company, in which the insurance agent interacts with the customer regarding a claim in a front-stage process. Backstage, the claim is handled by multiple employees (supported by technology) in sequence: a business clerk at the branch office, an underwriter at the head office, an issue clerk at the head office, and (last) a branch administrator who ultimately settles the claim with the customer. In this situation, it is important for backstage employees to understand how they are connected to the end user through other employees who are "internal customers." The customer may interact with backstage employees through remote channels (such as call centers), but they aren't visible. In some service organizations, the customer interacts with front stage and backstage employees—for example, sharing information—for the service to be delivered.

Service blueprinting can lead to innovative new services. For example, a cellphone app was recently launched that promises to help consumers quickly apply for a mortgage.

Organizations are interested in growing profitably, and—in recent years—highly innovative services have created lucrative new markets in developed economies. For example, eBay Inc. and Google emerged in 1996 and 1998, respectively, and quickly became top-ranked American companies.[6] eBay created a new service by bringing buyers and sellers together in a novel electronic marketplace, whereas Google created a new process for delivering information to people over the Internet. Notably, both organizations are capital intensive, rather than people-intensive, so that they have been able to achieve economies of scale. However, service innovation has also created profitable new markets in conventional people-intensive industries, such as Starbucks transformation of the "coffee shop experience" through superior employee and operational performance.

Multichannel Management

The number of channels that organizations can use interchangeably to provide service has proliferated due to technology. More than 80 percent of retailers are multichannel.[7] Consumers may browse or search for information online from a variety of sources and then purchase a product through a bricks and mortar store—or vice versa. Moreover, services can be delivered or consumed through different channels than they were acquired. For example, business customers can obtain service from private networks, the cloud, remote, or in-person interactions, customized solutions, or network partners. Although Dell Inc. is known for its online store, it has 170,000 channel partners. In the business press, the term "omni-channel" retailing has arisen to describe how multichannel retailing reflects the complexity of consumers' channel usage and experiences.[8]

Research has found that traditional and technology-mediated channels work together to influence customers' satisfaction with their entire experience.[9] There is evidence that introducing new channels induces sales growth due to increased loyalty, self-selection, or marketing efforts.[10] However, a few studies suggest that, despite multichannel service organizations gaining more sales than comparable service organizations operating with a single channel, they may suffer in terms of profitability, customer service, and customer retention either owing to duplication or cannibalization of existing channels.[11] More research is required on the performance of channel additions to reconcile these conflicting findings.

Another challenge of the proliferation of channels is that the organization is faced with large amounts of noisy data. For example, GE uses big data analytics to predict maintenance needs for its equipment. Operational data from sensors on its machinery—such as jet engines, turbines, and medical scanners—is analyzed for patterns that predict parts failure and downtime. In addition, real-time analytics enable GE machines to adapt continually and improve efficiency. Hence, GE is managing vast amounts of machine-generated data, along with data generated by service teams and customer centers. In this situation, GE's goal is to turn the unified data generated by people and machines into useable knowledge that can improve the customer experience and create efficiencies in service delivery.

Customer Experiences in Different Channels

Organizations create customer experiences in many different channels, including sales teams, field service teams, customer care centers, traditional stores, online stores, mobile apps, remote online services, and so forth.

Customers can use channels as substitutes or complements to accomplish their goals. Moreover, multiple channels have the potential to enhance the customer experience—by creating a portfolio of touchpoints—and (consequently) the benefits provided to the customer, thereby building loyalty and increased service usage. For this reason, channels can't be operated as functional silos. The customer experience must be consistent across channels—even though it will not be identical.

Channels are differentially effective in delivering an excellent customer experience. For example, consider shopping channels. Customers derive utilitarian value from browsing, searching, comparing prices, and creating assortments of products—as well as from acquiring products. They may also seek hedonic value from their channel experiences, such as fun, an adventure, or an opportunity to socialize. Thus, shoppers' channel preferences and usage patterns will depend on their shopping goals and past experiences—as well as on channel benefits, attributes, and capabilities.[12]

Early studies of channel experiences focused on business customers' experiences with sales channels and consumers' experiences with store channels—so the emphasis was on search and purchase activities. With the advent of electronic channels, many studies sought to identify channel benefits, attributes, and capabilities that might apply to all online shopping experiences. (An added complication is that customers frequently use their mobile phones to access online channels, where a retailer's mobile channel may be different, perhaps simplified, when compared with its full-service website.) Experiential attributes of online channels include: convenience, informativeness, merchandising, site or channel design (store atmospherics or website aesthetics), financial security, personalization, usability, and customer service.[13] This list is a reasonably good start for most organizations. However, there isn't a comprehensive list of channel attributes that is relevant to customer experiences in any channel. The channel benefits, attributes, and capabilities that are salient to the customer's experience will depend on her goals.[14]

Location-based services, such as Foursquare, are delivered by mobile phones as well as through kiosks, video displays, and other touchpoints. A key concern of managers is that shoppers primarily use their mobile telephones for search, so they can easily make comparisons—especially price comparisons—with competitors at the time of purchase. However, customers search for diverse kinds of information depending on their context (e.g., location, weather), product category, current experience, and so forth. The role of context is especially important because (as previously discussed) consumers' goals and emotions frame how the customer views her experience. Interestingly, access to diverse kinds of information at the purchase location can diminish the role that price plays in the purchase decision. A recent study of 2.5 million customers found that they search at many points in time—such as during consumption—not just directly prior to purchase.[15] The emergence of location-based services has also been disruptive in B2B contexts, as well as B2C contexts.

***Point to Ponder*:** The customer experience building blocks described in Chapter 4 should apply to any channel experience. Moreover, the unique online and mobile channel attributes are likely to also influence the channel experience. With this background, make a list of your organization's key channels. For each channel, list the key factors influencing the customer experience. How are the channels the same? Different? How does your organization ensure consistency in the customer experience across channels?

Channels Create Value for Organizations

The role of channels varies across organizations and industries, as well as depending on customer factors. From an organization's standpoint, some channels are strong at customer acquisition but weak at retention or vice versa—where the strength of a channel depends on the characteristics of the channel, consumer, product, and service.[16] Organizations should customize the channel experience to consumer needs, preferences, and usage patterns. Hence, the multichannel environment can be complex for organizations to understand and navigate. Moreover, sometimes an organization uses network partners or intermediaries (which may or may not be visible to the consumer) as channels. In these situations, customer behavior is difficult to track, model, and understand.

An integrated database is crucial to managing service operations and channels to design and deliver a superior customer experience. According to McKinsey Global Institute, the use of big data is becoming a key way for organizations to compete.[17]

> We estimate that a retailer embracing big data has the potential to increase its operating margin by more than 60%. We have seen leading retailers such as Tesco use big data to capture market share from local competitors, and many other examples abound in industries such as financial services.

A second study from IBM suggests that that organizations with mature business analytics can optimize resource allocation; the report estimates that they experience 20 times more profit growth.[18]

A key challenge facing service organizations is that there is no "one size fits all" strategy or set of rules to guide organizations on how to "lock-in" searching customers so that they purchase and use their services. However, there are some guidelines on how service organizations can identify and create cross-channel synergies. Researchers have identified five activities that can help organizations manage the multichannel environment more effectively.[19]

1. Managers should have a 360° view of the customer experience (both online and offline). This perspective requires the organization to integrate its data by matching customer records across channels.
2. Organizations must have a deep, as well as a broad, understanding of customer behavior—including how customers use channels to accomplish different purposes.
3. Organizations must rigorously evaluate their channels' benefits and capabilities and design channels to match customer needs.
4. Organizations must rethink how they allocate resources across channels to serve customers effectively.
5. Managers must coordinate channel strategies—they cannot be managed independently—so as to achieve seamless and consistent service.

Recovering from Service Failures

Service failures and recovery efforts have an important influence on customers' decisions about whether or not to continue their relationship with the organization. In an oft-repeated expression, Jan Carlzon,[20] President and CEO of Scandinavian Airlines, called them "moments of truth" for customer-focused organizations. Research indicates that service failures and failed recoveries are a leading cause of customer switching behavior.[21] A traditional rule of thumb used to be that customers who have experienced a service failure will tell nine or ten other people about it.[22] However, in recent years, savvy consumers have leveraged the Internet to reach a wide audience with their complaints, using sites such as Planet Feeback.com and uGetHeard.com. Some sites help consumers construct a complaint letter or lodge a complaint with a third party, such as an insurance commission, a government agency, the Better Business Bureau. They may also sell reports to companies. Social networking websites, such as MySpace or personal blogs, are widely used by people to share their attitudes and options. Consequently, the word-of-mouth repercussions of a service failure cannot be underestimated.

Managers must acknowledge that service failures will inevitably occur—even in organizations that are famed for their superior customer experiences—so employees must be trained and provided with resources to respond to them. There is a dangerous myth that service failures create opportunities to dazzle the customer with an excellent recovery—and strengthen relationships between the organization and its customers. This phenomenon is called "the service recovery paradox." Yes, this paradox is *occasionally* observed for a specific customer experience. However, most firms can't consistently deliver an excellent recovery, so it is far better to avoid service failure in the first place—and be prepared to deliver an excellent recovery when needed.[23] As a general rule, employees should:[24]

1. Offer an apology;
2. Act fast;
3. Offer a remedy or recovery that "matches" the service failure; and
4. Fix the process, as well as the problem.

These recommendations may seem rather straightforward, but each has subtle nuances that arise during implementation, as discussed in the following.

Offer an Apology

In many organizations, a key challenge for managers is recognizing that a service failure has occurred because the vast majority of customers do not complain. People are more likely to complain when:

- They view the problem as severe;
- They have suffered a financial loss;
- They are knowledgeable about the product;
- They are knowledgeable about how to complain; and
- The cost of complaining is low.

How can service employees know that a service failure has occurred and an apology is necessary?

- Employees can be trained to recognize a service failure. Customers can express negative emotions using distinct patterns of facial, postural, vocal, and verbal cues corresponding to anger, disappointment, and anxiety. Some people are adept at recognizing these emotions, and managers can use behavioral interviewing techniques to identify them and then hire them as employees.
- If such cues are not easily recognized, organizations should make it easy for customers to complain—usually using multiple methods. Customers may send complaints via Twitter, e-mail on the company website, 800 telephone numbers, suggestion boxes, and so forth.
- Organizations are developing models that identify failures based on analyses of social media data in real time and sometimes—using internal data—they are able to predict failures before they happen.

When they recognize a service failure, many employees—in their desire to act quickly—forget to apologize and immediately attempt to solve the customer's apparent problem. For example, a business traveler experiences a long delay when checking in to her hotel—and the receptionist initiates their conversation by saying "Do you have a reservation?" rather than greeting her and apologizing for the delay. For a minor process failure, such as a short delay in service, customers are frequently satisfied with an apology and require no other compensation.

Act Fast

The appropriate response to a particular service failure depends on the *type* of service failure the customer has experienced. Failures can be categorized into two general types: outcome failures that involve *what* customers actually receive from the service and process failures that involve *how* the service is delivered to customers (where it may be deficient or flawed in some way). Outcome failures typically create economic losses for the customer, such as a late delivery of parts that brings a manufacturer's assembly line to a halt or a business traveler "bumped" from an overbooked flight who misses an important client meeting. Process failures have social or symbolic consequences, such as when an employee is inattentive or discourteous, or a small error in an invoice erodes a purchasing manager's trust in a supplier.

Customers are more likely to be satisfied with a quick resolution of a process failure. Remarkably, customers who have experienced minor process failures are frequently satisfied by actions that have no cost to the organization, such as providing an *immediate* apology and *quickly* remedying the problem (e.g., moving a hotel guest to a nonsmoking room). This research finding can be rather startling to managers who believe that people require monetary compensation. Consumers are sometimes offered gift vouchers (e.g., for a restaurant meal or a movie) when a sincere apology and a rapid response would have satisfied them. As discussed under *Business Analytics*, it is sometimes possible to use predictive models to identify when service failures are likely to take place and prevent them. For example, airlines study weather patterns and sometimes alter flight schedules to avoid delays or cancellations.

Match the Recovery to the Failure

In general, recovery efforts that *specifically* address the loss suffered due to a service failure are more likely to restore the relationship between the customer and the organization than standardized solutions.[25] In other words, organizations should seek to respond with customized actions that "match" the type of failure that has occurred, so that (ultimately) the customer will view the recovery to be fair or just. Thus, customers who experience outcome failures will usually require monetary compensation or its equivalent.[26] Whereas a customer who has experienced an interactional service failure (such as poor or inattentive service from an employee) may consider a sincere apology and a gesture that conveys respect (e.g., when a hotel sends flowers or a fruit basket to a guest room).

What is an appropriate compensation? In some situations, employees can simply ask a customer how she would like the failure to be resolved—their suggestions are frequently quite reasonable. Abuse of this practice is avoided when repeat complainers are easily identified. Or, market research can be used to establish guidelines for how to respond to the most common types of service failures. Some organizations have been successful in empowering employees to use their judgment when they respond to service failures. They provide guidelines and suggestions, as well as a small budget to address such contingencies.

In all situations, the employee should:

1. Clarify with the customer the steps needed to solve the customer's problem;
2. Keep her informed about the resolution process; and
3. Follow up with the customer to ensure that the problem has been resolved to her satisfaction.

Organizations sometimes discover that problems, logged in their system as resolved, were never fully resolved from the customer's viewpoint or they have recurred. It can be helpful to establish a "single point of contact" for the customer so that the organization has a way to monitor and close the loop on problems. For this reason, many hotels have a "guest services" call button on in-room telephones, rather than separate buttons for different departments (such as housekeeping or reception). Public utilities have long been aware that repeated trouble reports from the same customer may indicate an underlying unresolved service failure. In such instances, organizations must persevere to regain customer goodwill. Frequently, business analytics or root cause analyses may help identify common service failures so that the service system can be improved for all customers.

It is very difficult to completely remedy a service failure, so there is a popular notion that service recovery requires "something extra" to create delight or outstanding service. This notion is likely to be true, at least from the organization's perspective. For example, a hotel that does not have a room available for a guest with a confirmed reservation must make an extensive effort to provide a solution that the customer considers equivalent to immediately honoring the reservation.

No Quick Fixes: Change Processes and Procedures

An organization is likely to discover innovations or improvements by carefully analyzing its service failures to better understand the customer experience. Hence, beyond responding to an individual customer's service failures, it is imperative that organizations track the incidence of different kinds of service failures and determine their root cause. Processes and procedures must be changed to forestall future occurrences of the same failure types, thereby reducing the costs of problem resolution and increasing customer retention (and consequently revenues). The financial rewards of doing so may not be apparent to everyone in the organization. Hence, managers frequently must start by measuring (in terms of foregone revenues) the cost of customers who are dissatisfied with their experience to their company and the benefits of higher levels of customer retention.[27] This is one reason why a deep understanding about how customer retention pays off for your organization is important (as discussed in Chapter 5).

Point to Ponder: Think about your organization or an organization you know well. Is it proactive in planning for occasional service failures by providing systems and processes for problem resolution or is it reactive?

Key Ideas

- Customers appreciate good design because human beings prefer integrity, completeness, and wholeness. So, for example, a customer experience must be delivered in a seamless fashion—

where technology and employees behave synergistically, as opposed to making conflicting demands on customers.

- Customers appreciate good design because people have an innate preference for symmetry and balance. They may feel uncomfortable when elements of the customer experience seem incongruous and don't fit with the brand promise or the current situation.
- Service design should begin with the new service concept: a detailed description of the customer needs to be satisfied, how they are to be satisfied, what is to be done for the customer, and how this is to be achieved.
- Channels can serve different functions. For example, new channels can open new markets to organizations—sometimes disrupting the marketplace (such as in the entertainment industry).
- Managers should consider what functions are performed during the customer experience and whether they can be separated. For example, customer provision of information and payment can often be separated from service delivery—leading to opportunities to design new services for new markets.
- Channels act as both substitutes and complements during the customer journey, so they must work together to provide seamless and consistent service. In many organizations, this goal poses challenges in managing information flows and sharing customer data.
- The organization must coordinate marketing, sales, human resources, operations (including supply chain and logistics functions), and information technology to design and deliver an excellent customer experience that builds relationships.
- A chief customer officer can play an important role in aligning all functions through the lens of the customer experience.
- Every organization, no matter how excellent, will sometimes provide unsatisfactory customer experiences. Organizations should be prepared to offer an apology, act fast, and offer a recovery that "matches" the failure.

- Service failures are an opportunity to learn and improve business processes for all customers.

Notes

1. Zeithaml and Bitner (2000); Magrath (1986).
2. Patrick and Hagtvedt (2011).
3. Lohr (2015).
4. Goldstein et al. (2002).
5. Grove and Fisk (1992).
6. Berry et al. (2006).
7. Neslin and Shankar (2009).
8. Verhoef, Kannan, and Inman (2015).
9. Van Birgelen, de Jong, and de Ruyter (2006).
10. Ansari, Mela, and Neslin (2008); Colgate and Danaher (2000); Kumar and Venkatesan (2005).
11. Lee and Grewal (2004).
12. Frambach, Roest, and Krishnan (2007).
13. Montoya-Weiss, Voss, and Grewal (2003); Szymanski and Hise (2000); Wolfinbarger and Gilly (2001).
14. Zeithaml, Parasuraman, and Malhotra (2000).
15. Daurer et al. (2015).
16. Van Birgelen, de Jong, and de Ruyter (2006); Dong, Swain, and Berger (2007).
17. Saran (2015).
18. Lavalle (2015).
19. Neslin et al. (2006).
20. Carlzon (1987).
21. Keaveney (1995).
22. Albrecht and Bradford (1990).
23. Smith and Bolton (1998).
24. Smith, Bolton, and Wagner (1999).
25. Smith, Bolton, and Wagner (1999).
26. Gilly and Gelb (1982).
27. Fornell and Wernerfelt (1987).

CHAPTER 8

Managing Partners, People, and Physical Evidence

People—network partners, employees, and customers—are central to the cocreation of customer experiences. In a customer-focused, knowledge-based marketplace, employees are critical to the design and delivery of services that lead to business success. For example, Google sets a high standard. Whether you're applying for an administrative assistant position or that of senior engineer, every candidate is screened by their potential boss, potential colleagues, a hiring committee, and finally Google CEO Larry Page.[1] Hence, this chapter begins by discussing four categories of people directly concerned with delivering effective service:

1. Customer contact personnel
2. Other employees
3. Network partners
4. Other customers

It also describes strategies for managing people, especially customer-facing employees.[2] Since employees play a critical role, the first half of this chapter discusses hiring, training, supporting and rewarding them—plus how to create a favorable service culture and climate within the organization.

The customer experience with an organization—and its people—is embedded in a physical environment, called a "servicescape." Servicescape refers to the physical environment at the service site, including ambient conditions (e.g., temperature, noise, lighting), spatial layout, and functionality (which influence crowding and participation), and signs, symbols, and other objects, including the design of technology.[3] With the emergence of the Internet of Things (IoT), it also includes objects that can communicate with each other—and with the customer—to enhance the service experience. Hence, the second half of this chapter describes how the servicescape influences the customer experience through three major categories of physical evidence:

1. Tangible cues that influence perceptions
2. Retail environments
3. Branding and communication

Customer Contact Personnel and Other Employees

Service personnel—that is, employees that have contact with customers—play an important role in the service experience because their appearance, attitudes, and behavior will influence customers' perceptions of the service and their behavior. In some industries, such as consulting or hairstyling, service personnel deliver the largest component of the service—and, from the customer's perspective, they embody the service. This situation is potentially rather dangerous because customers may be loyal to service personnel not the organization. Clients may follow consultants, account managers, or other professional service providers when they change jobs.

The social aspects of service experiences influence customer satisfaction and loyalty. For example, customers will be more satisfied with their experience when service personnel are friendly, knowledgeable, and provide personalized service. They also tend to be more satisfied when service personnel are satisfied with their jobs. Interestingly, empirical evidence in a bank setting shows that the influence of a poorly performing personal banker had a negative influence on customer loyalty that is more severe than the positive influence of an excellent personal banker.[4]

Social bonds are important in both business-to-business (B2B) and business-to-consumer (B2C) markets. Social bonds created by employee-delivered service have been shown to influence business customers' perceptions of the value provided by a large telecommunications company, whereas structural bonds created by financial or operational procedures have a stronger effect on customer satisfaction. In this way, social bonds have a subtle but profound effect on future purchase behavior.[5]

Service personnel are sometimes called "boundary-spanners" because they operate at the dividing line between front-stage and backstage operations. This position can be stressful because they must respond to the expectations of the customer and the service organization, where the two sets of expectations are not always consistent. In addition, their job requires them to display feelings (e.g., friendliness) that they may not always be genuine—especially when they are handling difficult situations.

Each employee is linked to the customer through the role she plays in creating and delivering service benefits. For example, a backstage delay by an insurance underwriter has a ripple effect through operations that ultimately affects the performance of the insurance agent and the insurance company from the customers' perspective. It can be difficult for employees to understand how their performance contributes to the customer's service experience. Companies must demonstrate to their employees how each of them serves an internal customer (i.e., a coworker) who is ultimately linked to an external customer.[6]

***Point to Ponder*:** How does your organization help each employee understand how he or she is linked (through other employees, systems, technology, and so forth to the external customer)?

Employees of Network Partners

The employees of an organizations' network partners are also relevant to the delivery of an effective customer experience. Some services (e.g., call or repair centers) can be outsourced, so that many customers may believe that they are interacting with an organization when they are (in fact) dealing with its supplier, which may be located almost anywhere in the world. For example, customer service centers, data management, engineering, medical, and financial services are increasingly outsourced so that organizations can focus on their core competencies. Many consumers have had the experience of discovering (much to their surprise.) that the representative handling their service request was located in another country, many time zones away. In such situations, it is imperative that the organization work closely with its supplier to deliver seamless service.

Organizations that deliver service through franchises, such as Best Western® Hotels and Resorts, must work closely with owner-operators to communicate customer expectations, develop service standards, evaluate service performance, and compare it with customers' perceptions of the service experience. It tracks process metrics for each aspect of a hotel stay: prearrival, arrival, guest stay, checkout, and postcheckout. Its attention to the customer experience has paid off. 1,808 Best Western hotels (55 percent of its properties) were honored with 2015 TripAdvisor Certificate of Excellence awards. In addition, 378 hotels received Hall of Fame recognition, signifying they have earned a Certificate of Excellence for the past five consecutive years.

Other Customers

In addition to the focal customer, other customers in the service environment can influence service delivery. This feature is especially noticeable when service experiences take place in a specific physical setting, such as hotels, restaurants, theaters, schools, hospitals, and offices. For example, hotel chains catering to business travelers have revised their family programs offering special services and activities for children. Starwood Hotels and Resorts Worldwide introduced new designer cribs at its Westin and Sheraton brands in 2001, but it didn't add a full children's program at all properties. Instead, a redesigned Kids Club was added to its family and leisure focused Westin brand in 2006—but not at Starwood brands and properties catering to business travelers.[7]

In B2B situations, customers who have similar needs, expectations, and behaviors can provide support to each other, thereby increasing the value provided by the service organization. Many organizations, such as Oracle or Apple, welcome the existence of user groups that interact physically at conferences and expositions, as well as online. Consumers also interact through online social networks or communities. Prominent social networking websites include: MySpace, Facebook (the United States), Bebo (UK), Cyworld (South Korea), and Mixi (Japan). These websites are viable businesses that create and capture value in a novel way: millions of people spend hours creating value by interacting with each other, thereby providing an audience for organizations who buy advertising space. Beyond the direct effects of advertising, users interact with each other about products—accelerating word-of-mouth effects.

Hiring People to Deliver Excellent Customer Experiences

Due to rapid changes in the marketplace, many organizations are building new capabilities—requiring highly skilled employees. For example, software engineers are in short supply in many markets in the United States. What is the solution? One solution is to look in unusual places and then work to be a preferred employer. For example, some companies have hired software engineers that work remotely from India and China. Other companies have developed strong ties with universities that graduate software engineers. Organizations can offer customized jobs, flexible work hours, and cafeteria benefits to satisfy the needs of different employee groups.

In the careers section of its website, Southwest Airlines proclaims: "Feel Free to Actually Enjoy What You Do." Southwest is a highly selective employer, hiring only a small percentage of the many people who apply for jobs. It competes for the best people, hires carefully, and screens out unsuitable employees during a probationary period. These are good policies for almost any organization, but especially for customer-focused, service-centric organizations. It is much easier for an organization to hire a person with a "servant's heart" than to inculcate the desire to serve. Some service organizations use behavioral interviewing techniques, so that they can identify and hire people with specific service competencies. For example, a potential Starbucks employee might be asked to role-play or to describe how she would handle certain customer service challenges. Or, if a manager wished to hire a customer call center representative, the first interview might be conducted by telephone to evaluate the potential employee's vocal qualities (clear speech, warm tone of voice).

At the same time, different employee jobs require different kinds of people, so different human resource strategies will be effective. In highly competitive labor markets, it is useful for managers to segment the employee market, just as she might segment its customers, and then develop a strong relationship with each group. Naturally, if a service organization wishes to be selective in this way, they must work to become a preferred employer. For example, Hai Di Lao, a hotpot restaurant chain in China, has overcome challenges to recruiting and retaining employees to serve as restaurant managers by offering them housing, schooling for their children, and trips abroad. Some organizations offer flexible work schedules and other benefits which (unlike compensation) competitors may find it difficult to match. Note that benefits, rather than compensation, may be very important. Long-distance truck drivers may value benefits that support their family's lives while they are away, whereas hotel workers on the night shift may value educational benefits that lead to career advancement.

Training to Develop People's Knowledge and Ability to Serve

After hiring the people who are willing to serve, the next step is to develop employees' knowledge and ability to serve. Ideally, managers should offer newly hired employees a comprehensive orientation to the entire organization, including its history, physical plant, service culture, employees, procedures, and customers. For example, Mayo Clinic orients all employees—even if they don't work directly with patients—to ensure that they understand how their jobs affect patient care.[8] Housekeeping staff must understand how sanitary conditions contribute to patient health. The business rationale for a comprehensive orientation is that almost any employee may come in contact with customers and (thus) represent the organization. Disney, a company that is known for its outstanding training programs, offers a comprehensive new hire orientation program for its "cast members." Equally important, it also offers a multitude of additional training opportunities, including computer skills, management and leadership, professional development, executive development, ethics, and integrity and diversity programs.

Classroom training is typically insufficient to train excellent service personnel. As a general rule, it is necessary to use *continuous, multiple methods* to develop skills (including interpersonal skills) and sustain a service culture. To many managers, this statement may seem unduly onerous ("When does the real work get done?"). However, there are numerous efficient training tools. Computerized training allows for the efficient transmission of new information. Managers can build opportunities for training and rehearsing new skills into routine operational activities. For example, supervisors can visit and coach employees as they perform their job.

Experiential learning is especially powerful for service providers, as it is in many contexts, so it is important to lead by example. Marriott Corporation offered a training program called "Seed and Lead," whereby hotel employees who demonstrated service excellence were eligible to be temporarily transferred to new hotels to serve as role models for newly hired employees. This policy served to recognize and reward outstanding employees, and to infuse best practices throughout the organization. After 13 years of tremendous growth, Alibaba's workforce had grown to over 23,000 in 2009. At that point, it turned its attention to human resource challenges: undertaking a structural reorganization and rethinking how it trained the 4,000 to 5,000 new employees it hired each year. In 2010, it started preparing its future leaders through job rotation and special "classes" led by Jack Ma, Chairman and CEO.[9]

***Point to Ponder*:** Think of an organization you know well. Does it seek to improve work processes used by employees? Does it discover more effective tools for employees?

Supporting People to Provide Excellent Service Experiences

The business rationale for supporting employees is very straightforward.

- Employees who are supported are more productive, more satisfied, and deliver excellent experiences to customers, thereby enhancing profitability.
- Research shows that, when employees give favorable reports on how they are trained, supervised, and supported, customers have favorable views of their experience.[10]
- Organizations are better able to cocreate excellent customer experiences when they have high levels of employee retention.
- Aligning frontline service employee behavior with an organization's brand positioning can positively influence customer's perceptions of the service experience—especially when brands are new to customers.[11]

Specifically, aligning employee behavior with the brand positioning requires employees to be fluent in conveying the brand message and authentic in how they deliver service. Consequently, numerous organizations have become highly successful by pursuing a differential advantage based on recruiting, training and supporting service personnel.

Case Study: ServiceMaster Creates a Favorable Service Climate by Supporting Employees

ServiceMaster provides building and lawn maintenance services to 10.5 million homes and businesses in the United States each year, through seven branded services such as Terminix, Merry Maids, Rescue Rooter, TruGreen, and ChemLawn. It is committed to the continuing development of each worker: training and supporting employees in their current job responsibilities, preparing them for continuous career growth, and providing opportunities to move up based on merit. This strategy translates into concrete support for workers, such as providing the best equipment (such as mops, lawn mowers, and chemical applicators) and training in how to use it, as well as educational support as workers move into management positions. A strategy that supports employees is equally applicable in high-technology industries that rely on engineers and service technicians. Supporting employees is consistent with a management philosophy that treats people with dignity, fairness, and respect.

Employees should be able to rely on the organization (and its managers) to communicate expectations regarding role performance, as well as reinforce and reward desired behaviors. A good exemplar of these practices is Southwest Airlines, a company that encourages employee involvement and teamwork (through cross-training), and promotes a willingness to make the job fun. Although its business model is clearly different from the competition, one key reason for its success is that employees are not only supported but also given the freedom to serve customers without getting into trouble. Southwest is willing to fire customers who abuse their employees—and have stated this position publicly on many occasions. As a result, Southwest Airlines is the only consistently profitable airline in an industry that has undergone considerable change.

***Point to Ponder*:** Abercrombie & Fitch has received considerable press attention for its policies regarding the "look" and behavior of its employees. What are the opportunities and pitfalls of managing the fit between frontline employee behavior and brand positioning?

Recognition and Rewards Tied to Excellent Customer Experiences

Starbucks operates more than 20,000 stores worldwide. Its growth is primarily fueled by the interactions that its baristas (called "partners") have with customers. Starbucks views its partners as a key competitive advantage in the marketplace. Unlike some classic brands (e.g., Coca-Cola), its partners make emotional connections with customers during the service experience every day. Hence, Starbucks baristas drive customer acquisition and retention through service. Recently, the company has increased its training of baristas on how to "make every moment right" to ensure an excellent customer experience. This strategy is sustainable in the long run because it is so difficult to imitate and implement best practices for managing employees. Starbucks' story provides a compelling example of why organizations should measure employee performance and reward employees who create excellent service experiences. In some instances, it is necessary to recognize or reward service teams, as well as individuals, to ensure that appropriate coordination of internal processes takes place.

It will be necessary to use multiple ways of measuring the customer experience including internal performance metrics (orders filled, billing errors), external performance metrics (activity-driven survey ratings, retention statistics), and financial metrics (contribution margin per customer). It is especially important to recognize and reward discretionary effort—where employees go that extra mile to provide a superior service experience to internal or external customers. Recognition acknowledges employee excellence and provides role models for coworkers to emulate. Naturally, recognition and reward systems must be tied to internal and external performance metrics that are within employees' control.

One novel way of recognizing employees or teams involves gamification—that is, introducing elements of game playing (such as competition and point scoring) to business activities. For example, the U.S. Army uses games in training, as well as in attracting recruits with a virtual army experience. Games should be designed so that the player's goals overlap with the organization's goals. Games should be motivating, fun, and emotionally rewarding. For example, sales or service teams can compete for the highest score, where points are awarded for achieving specific business objectives, and participants receive badges and other social status symbols on social media websites.

This chapter has emphasized service-centered tactics for managing employees through hiring, training procedures, support systems, and rewards. However, the effective management of employees requires service-centered *strategies*, as well as *tactics*. At a strategic level, organizations must "walk the walk," as well as "talk the talk." Organizations should begin by clearly communicating its vision and values.

Case Study: Publix Supermarkets Recognizes and Rewards Its Employees

Publix Supermarkets, Inc. is one of the United States' largest regional supermarket chains. It was founded in 1930 and has never had a layoff. It is a majority employee-owned company, with a tuition reimbursement program. *Fortune* magazine has listed it as one of the "Best Companies to Work For" every year since 1998. On walking into any supermarket, a customer will immediately see the names and photos of all employees featured on the wall. At Publix, employees are intrinsically motivated, as well as extrinsically motivated through its compensation, benefits, and reward systems. Naturally, its employees are likely to "buy in" to the organization's vision because they are owners with input into how the service strategy is developed and implemented.

Service Culture and Climate

Managing people entails the creation of an organizational culture that values the excellent service experiences for both internal and external customers.[12] An organizational culture is created by developing a pattern of shared values, beliefs, and norms that give people meaning and provide them with rules for behavior within the organization.[13] *When a service culture exists, employees instinctively know how to handle service challenges even when there is no relevant policy or procedure.* A service culture takes time to develop because it must be infused throughout the organization and its norms must be internalized by organizational members. Its development requires formal processes that value good service, such as programs linking recognition and rewards to the delivery of excellent service experiences, as well as informal processes. A superior service culture can originate highly visible role models, such as a founding chief executive officer who is highly visible in demonstrating her commitment to service. However, many organizations have emerged from financial difficulties to become an industry leader by creating a service-centered culture. YRC Worldwide (formerly Yellow Roadway) developed a service-centered strategy that improved its financial performance and led to it being named the most admired trucking company.[14]

Case Study: Zappos Creates a Service Culture

The astounding growth of Zappos, the online shoe and clothing store, was fueled by its powerful service culture. Although most sales take place online, customers typically telephoned its call center at least once at some point.[15] Each call was considered an opportunity to make an emotional connection with a customer and build the Zappos brand. In early 2004, the company was having trouble finding the right employees to staff its expanding call center. To obtain access to high caliber employees, CEO Tony Hsieh's solution was to move the entire company (not just the call center) from San Francisco to Las Vegas. Why? The values embodied in Zappos service culture indicated that decoupling its call center from company headquarters didn't make sense. Customer service was its core competency. It was a revenue generator not a cost center. Employees weren't evaluated on the basis of productivity measures such as "handle time" because customers with great service experiences marketed the Zappos brand through word of mouth. By keeping the company headquarters and the call center together, Zappos was preserving its service culture and staying close to the customer. Amazon acquired Zappos in 2009 under arrangements designed to preserve its service culture and reward employees.

Recent research suggests that organizations can create a favorable service climate through:

1. Leadership—including a commitment to everyday management activities that improve customer experiences;
2. Human resource management practices—including high-performance-oriented practices; and
3. Systems support from operations, marketing, information technology, and other functions—especially that leads to internal service quality for employees.

A favorable service climate is characterized by "a 'positive' and 'strong' shared perception that policies, practices, and procedures, as well as the behaviors that are rewarded, supported, and expected, focus on service."[16] Employee engagement is a necessary but not a sufficient condition for a favorable service climate. Moreover, a favorable service climate goes beyond the positive service orientation of an individual employee, team, or work unit. A *strong* service climate implies that employees have a shared view of the service climate. A *favorable* service climate positively influences employees' role performance and customer-focused helping behaviors, as well as directly influencing customers' perceptions of quality, satisfaction, and self-reports of loyalty.

Physical Evidence: The Servicescape

The customer experience is primarily intangible, so it may seem counter-intuitive to discuss physical evidence. However, as discussed in Chapter 4, the customer experience is embedded in a rich context at a specific point in time. Indeed, most service organizations, such as hotels, stores, and airlines, make substantial investments in physical plant to provide a superior service experience. For example, at a spa, the lighting, music, and scented warm air provide a relaxing atmosphere for the delivery of spa services. The customer doesn't necessarily notice each atmospheric element; she simply makes a holistic evaluation of the service experience. For example, Lufthansa decided to install humidifiers in its first-class cabins on some routes to better serve lucrative long-haul customers who pay premium fares. Customers may not notice the exact humidity levels, but they are likely to feel better in subtle ways. For this reason, organizations must carefully balance aesthetics and functionality within the servicescape. For example, ambiguous physical cues that signal innovativeness may also create a sense of uncertainty that leads to lack of trust.[17]

The servicescape is defined as the physical environment at the service site, including ambient conditions (e.g., temperature, noise, lighting), spatial layout and functionality (which influence crowding and participation), and signs, symbols and other objects, including the design of technology.[18] It includes peripheral objects such as invoices and employee uniforms. It also includes objects that can communicate with each other via the IoT—and with the customer—to enhance the service experience. For example, some consumers already have a smart thermostat in their home, soon they may own a smart appliance or a smart car.

Tangible Cues Influence Perceptions of the Service Experience

The organization's tangible cues should be consistent with its positioning in the market place and its service brand promise.[19] For example, Wal-Mart Stores tested a new uniform, a blue polo shirt, and khaki pants, to replace the blue smocks and vests (embroidered with the phrase "How Can I Help You?") worn by its 1.3 million workers in the United States. When the test took place in 100 stores, a *New York Times* reporter speculated that Wal-Mart's test of a new preppy wardrobe might indicate that the organization is "drifting away" from a focus on its core customer segment, members of the working class.[20] In addition, tangibles convey subtle cues that influence the customer's perceptions of their experience.

Case Study: Lowe's Leverages Servicescape to Improve Customer Experience

Lowe's, a home improvement store, displays many products in usage settings similar to how they would be used in customers' homes (e.g., outdoor patio displays with cookout equipment). Its goal is to enable the customer to interact with the products and experience them prior to purchase, fostering engagement activities. By improving the customer experience, it intends to drive growth. In addition, Lowe's is experimenting with a Holoroom, retail service robots, and in-store 3D scanning. In this way, it is preparing for the day that technology infuses the retail customer experience. It is also signaling to consumers that they can trust Lowe's to provide relevant customer experiences in the future. Note how all these strategies and tactics align with the customer experience building blocks in Figure 4.1.

Professional services include accountants, lawyers, architects, engineers, consultants, doctors, and so forth. These services are particularly challenged on how to cocreate an excellent customer experience due to the intangible nature of their professional expertise. Over the past 25 years, restrictions on professional services ability to use traditional methods of promotion and advertising have eased considerably in the United States. However, service providers in these industries have quickly learned that superior service experience—that differentiates the provider from the competition—includes attention to many aspects of the servicescape that can influence service quality, such as telephone systems, office layout, furnishings, and lighting—as well as management of processes and people as discussed earlier.

Retail Environments

Diverse organizations—including retail stores, amusement parks, hospitals, and airports—have studied how changes in spatial layout and functionality can influence traffic patterns, crowding, and waiting times, thereby influencing the customer experience and (ultimately) service usage. Some hospitals, such as Emory University Hospital's Rollins Pavilion, provide private rooms and suites, in-room dining (similar to restaurants in hotels), spa-like services, and other fee-based amenities. An office supply store replaced an "aisle grid" with a "racetrack" that looped around the store—ensuring that shoppers could find and purchase destination product categories. Chang, K. ambient conditions and symbolic objects have become increasingly important to supermarkets, which are attempting to differentiate themselves. For example, Trader Joe's has created a tropical décor that successfully sells inexpensive private label products within an exciting shopping environment. Wegmans Food Markets Inc., a regional supermarket chain in the Northeastern United States, has been very successful by offering superior service and a diverse product assortment that includes foods prepared in the store—with appealing scents and sights to tempt shoppers. These retailers encourage shoppers to shop longer and buy more products. Online retailers have the same goals. In Internet parlance, they try to create "sticky" websites.

Retail environments, such as shopping malls, are particularly interesting examples of the role of servicescape.[21] Shopping malls have suffered from intensive competition from new shopping alternatives (the Internet, category killers, discount stores, and factory outlets), the saturation of locations in urban areas, and changes in consumers' shopping behavior. Mall managers and retailers have developed strategies that differentiate them from the competition by providing a unique shopping experience with diverse products and services. These strategies go beyond improvements in spatial layout and functionality to reduce crowding and ensure that customers spend more time at the mall.

Different segments of shoppers consider different aspects of the servicescape to be important. Sony Corporation, a leading manufacturer of consumer electronics, operates a retail store chain in Canada. At one time, it tried to broaden its appeal to women shoppers by introducing a scent that blends orange and vanilla with a hint of cedar wood into its 37 stores.[22] The organization's underlying (and probably mistaken) premise was that the scent would influence their spending patterns.

Branding and Communications

An organization's branding and communications strategy delivers a brand promise regarding the customer experience that must be matched by its execution. For example, consumers expect Apple to produce innovative, well-designed products and Disney to be family friendly. Tools, such as the *Gap Model*, are useful in ensuring that the expectations created by the brand promise are met. It is important that expectations aren't set too high (because customers can be disappointed) or set too low (because customers will try competitors first). The organization's goal should be consistency. An expert on branding has developed a "Brand Report Card" or checklist to help managers evaluate the strength of their communications. In studying these criteria, it is important to remember that the manager's assessment should be based on *the brand's meaning to customers*, not the brand as it is seen from within the organization. The brand will have meaning based on how it is seen in the marketplace (i.e., all customers), as well as personal meaning to individual customers. (For example, a couple were married at the Coca Cola museum because the brand held special meaning for them.) Customers' connections with brands involve their social identities. Brand meaning results from these connections.

The manager is tasked with evaluating the following:[23]

- The brand excels at delivering the benefits of the experience that customers truly desire.
- The brand stays relevant to future needs.
- The pricing strategy is based on customers' perceptions of fairness, satisfaction, and value.
- The brand is properly positioned vis-à-vis the competition.
- The brand is consistent across communications mix and over time.
- The brand portfolio and hierarchy make sense (e.g., tiered value offerings).
- The brand makes use of and coordinates a full repertoire of service activities to build brand equity and corporate reputation.
- The organization's employees understand what the brand means to customers (i.e., a favorable service culture and climate).
- The brand is given proper support and that support is maintained over the long run (through R&D, support spending, etc.).

In considering this checklist, it is important to remember that brand equity is not completely under the control of the organization. Since organizations and customers cocreate experiences (Chapter 3), the brand's promise and brand identity will be understood in different ways by different people.[24] Beyond the meaning ascribed by individuals, many brands are the center of user or brand communities that cocreate new experiences and meanings. With the rise in social media (Chapter 2), customer-generated brand stories have become pervasive and highly influential. The importance of social media to the brand will depend on the nature of consumer-brand relationships (e.g., brand attachments), whether the brand is publicly (versus privately) consumed, and market factors (e.g., competition, product harm crises). For these reasons, experts recommend a network-oriented approach to branding activities. Hence, the management of branding and communications must start from a deep understanding of the customer experience (Chapter 4). It also requires a coordinated approach to cocreating experiences with customers – across functional activities and channels (Chapter 7).

These criteria are especially important when there is a single corporate brand for the organization, rather than a "house of brands." It is also important to remember that employees monitor and evaluate organizational branding and communications. They will be influenced by the brand promise, as well.[25] Last, given the increased visibility of consumer-to-consumer (C2C) interactions, it is important that the brand is relevant and trustworthy in carrying out its corporate social responsibilities.

Given the ascendance of new media, organizations recognize that brand communications are two-way communications (B2C, C2B, and C2C) not one-way communications (B2C). Moreover, neither all brand communications are controlled by the brand—nor is it possible to respond to them all. For this reason, it is important to systematically consider how the brand sets expectations for customers (i.e., the brand promise), accurately reflects the customer experience and reinforces other elements of service design and delivery. A special concern is to ensure that some elements of brand communications are not incongruent with the customer experience.

***Point to Ponder*:** What is your organization's service promise? How does its servicescape and brand communications reinforce its promise? Are all elements consistent with your organization's positioning and strategy? Are all elements consistent with the customer experience?

Key Ideas

- Manage partners, people, and physical evidence (including technology) so that they are congruent with the design and execution of the customer experience.
- Customer-facing employees play a critical role as boundary spanners. They sometimes embody the organization to the customer.
- Hiring, training, supporting, and rewarding customer-facing employees requires a customer-focused, service-centric perspective. For example, recognition and rewards should be tied to excellent customer experiences.
- Employees of network partners and other customers can also influence customer experiences, so they must be considered in designing service experiences.
- When a service culture exists, employees instinctively know how to handle service challenges when there is no relevant policy or procedure.
- A favorable service climate is characterized by a positive and strong shared perception that policies, practices, and procedures, as well as the behaviors that are rewarded, supported, and expected, focus on serving customers.
- A favorable service climate can be created through specific leadership capabilities, human resource management practices, and system support.
- The servicescape is defined as the physical environment at the service site, including ambient conditions, spatial layout and functionality, signs, symbols, technology, and other objects (e.g., employee uniforms).

- Servicescape principles apply to all channels (online or offline), as well as all branding and communications.

Notes

1. Bock (2015).
2. Schneider and Bowen (1985, 1993, 2010).
3. Bitner (1992, 1993).
4. Colgate and Danaher (2000).
5. Bolton, Smith, and Wagner (2003).
6. Berry (1981).
7. Elliott Christopher (2006).
8. Berry and Bendapudi (2003).
9. Limin (2012).
10. Schneider and Bowen (1985).
11. Sirianni et al. (2013).
12. Schneider (1986).
13. Bowen and Schneider (2014).
14. *Fortune* (2006).
15. Hsieh (2010).
16. Bowen and Schneider (2014, 6).
17. Patrick and Hagtvedt (2011).
18. Bitner (1992).
19. Bitner (1995).
20. Barbaro (2006).
21. Baker et al. (2002); Michon, Chebat, and Turley (2005); Spangenberg, Crowley, and Henderson (1996).
22. Caplan (2006).
23. Keller (2000).
24. Gensler et al. (2013).
25. Gilly and Wolfinbarger (1998).

CHAPTER 9

Globalization: Learning to Tailor the Customer Experience to New Markets

In Lewis Carroll's *Through the Looking Glass,* Alice finds herself running alongside the Red Queen (a chess piece), but no matter how fast they run, they never pass anything. Finally, they stop:

> Alice looked round her in great surprise. "Why, I do believe we've been under this tree the whole time. Everything's just as it was."
>
> "Of course it is," said the Queen. "What would you have it?"
>
> "Well, in our country," said Alice, still panting a little, "you'd generally get to somewhere else—if you ran very fast for a long time as we've been doing."
>
> "A slow sort of country." said the Queen. "Now, here, you see, it takes all the running you can do, to keep in the same place. If you want to get somewhere else, you must run at least twice as fast as that."

Alice feels that she is racing very fast—only to learn that she must run much faster to reach her goal—and to beat the Red Queen!

This incident provides an analogy for how organizations must compete in a changing marketplace. They must be attentive to the changes in the landscape, including changes in customer preferences and competitor actions. A learning organization translates observation into action—moving quickly to beat the competition. A learning organization will have processes to foster innovation and continuous improvement in the customer experience—so that its offerings serve customers better than competitors and create strong relationships with them.

Managers inevitably grapple with the problem of moving from observation—measuring and analyzing the customer experience—to action. This book has described many ways to overcome this challenge. These activities should take place on an ongoing basis. For example, innovation and improvement teams drawn from different functional areas within the organization can meet regularly to identify new ways to coordinate, design, and deliver excellent customer experiences.

Organizational learning is especially important in the globalized marketplace. Since the customer experience is context-specific, the organization must learn about customers and adapt their service strategies. This chapter:

1. Identifies some of the challenges of globalization;
2. Discusses how people's preferences and behavior differ across nations and cultures;
3. Identifies implications of globalization for managing the customer experience; and
4. Outlines some future directions and challenges for organizations.

Challenges of Globalization

Regional unification (the European Union, the North American Free Trade Agreement, the proposed Trans-Pacific Partnership) has reduced—but not eliminated—national differences that impeded trade, including laws, regulations, subsidies, copyrights, and patents. For this reason, the global service sector is growing exponentially relative to the industrial goods sector as organizations have begun to compete in adjacent markets and seek lower labor costs.[1]

Consequently, global brands have become increasingly important to organizations and to consumers. A global brand's country-of-origin often conveys important information to customers. German car manufacturers may benefit from Germany's reputation for high-quality engineering. Italian leather goods makers may benefit from Italy's reputation for bespoke fashion. However, some experts argue that people ascribe certain characteristics to global brands—simply due to their success in the global marketplace. Specifically, global brands seem to promise quality, social responsibility, and access to a global culture.[2] Organizations must grapple with these expectations—and how to meet or shape them.

Managers face pressing strategic questions about global brands. How should service offerings be designed and marketed? Should offerings be introduced sequentially or simultaneously into new markets? Under what circumstances will customers pay a premium for customized services? Services frequently require intensive customer contact—yet customers rely on diverse signals to evaluate the customer experience—so questions about customization and pricing are especially difficult to resolve. Unlike goods, customer experiences cannot be resold, so customer-focused, service-centered organizations are likely to be less concerned with the diverting of sales across national boundaries.

Should the organization enter a foreign market through exporting, licensing, joint venture, or sole venture? A sole venture may allow the organization to better control service quality levels. How should the organization take into account differences in the competitive environment, including trade practices and regulatory conditions? (e.g., Starbucks has acquired stores previously operated by franchisees in China to ensure a consistent customer experience.) What should be the level of resource commitments, including investments in technology?

How People's Preferences and Behavior Differ Across Nations and Cultures

Much of what scholars know about management was discovered through studies conducted in developed Western countries, often the United States. Although knowledge about management outside the United States is growing rapidly, it may not generalize to other nations or cultures (or vice versa.) This dilemma influences every aspect of organizational conduct in global markets. For example, research conducted in developed Western countries shows that formalization and centralization of decision making tends to have a negative effect on an organization's market orientation, reducing customer focus.[3] However, in countries with a cultural hierarchy and lower education levels (e.g., Zimbabwe), moderate levels of formalization and centralization stimulate information acquisition and dissemination and create customer focus—by helping employees better understand their roles.[4] Beyond cross-cultural and cross-national differences, different organizations have different organizational cultures that must also be taken into account.

International services are defined as services conducted across national boundaries and (frequently) different cultures. They must be customized (to some degree) to different contexts. National characteristics, as well as cultural norms and beliefs, have a strong influence on how consumers' preferences evolve and on how they think and act. For example, a study of financial services showed that individualist countries, such as the United States, should place greater emphasis on personal legitimacy of service employees than on institutional legitimacy. This finding means focusing more on training, motivating, and empowering service employees to actively take roles, and display confidence. In contrast, in collectivist countries, such as India, service employees should emphasize building institutional legitimacy to signal credibility.[5]

Case Study: Kentucky Fried Chicken in China

Kentucky Fried Chicken (KFC) was once the most famous international brand in China. KFC achieved its rapid growth by introducing a range of new Chinese-style fast food, involving chicken rolls and soup to match the tastes of Chinese consumers. In 2000, the A.C. Nielsen Company reported that 45 percent of people surveyed in 30 major Chinese cities said they had tasted KFC at least once. By 2004, KFC had 1,000 outlets—compared with McDonald's Corporation's 560 outlets. In an attempt to catch up, McDonald's decided to almost double its outlets in China before the 2008 Beijing Olympics (which it helped sponsor) to drive customer engagement. It also signed up Chinese basketball star Yao Ming of the Houston Rockets as an official spokesperson. In addition to competitive threats, KFC suffered setbacks due to quality and food-safety problems in the poultry supply chain in China. These events eroded Chinese consumers' trust in the service brand. By 2015, KFC had lost its preeminent position in the quick-service restaurant industry in China. Yum Brands announced it would spin off a separate unit in China to revive its service brands. Time will tell if it will be successful.

Implications of Globalization for Managing the Customer Experience

National and cultural differences can include language, values and attitudes, manners and customs, material culture, aesthetics, and customer behavior. For this reason, customers from different nations and cultures may place different values on an aspect of the service experience—requiring customization of services. On the other hand, the emergence of a global marketplace—fueled by regional unification, standardization of investment and production strategies, and increasing flows of information, labor, and technology across borders—has led to the emergence of customer groups with common preferences that transcend national borders and cultures. For example, a cross-national segment of business customers for an IT service supplier might place roughly equal value on response time—which could be delivered by providing standardized 24/7 customer service at regional call centers. Such a standardization strategy can be very tempting because it reduces operational costs (by eliminating redundant efforts across nations) and effectively allocates the organization's resources. From a practical standpoint, global service organizations must calculate the benefits and costs of customization versus standardization of specific service attributes.[6]

A successful strategy for global marketing of services depends on the organization's ability to segment its markets so that uniform decisions can be applied to specific groups that exist horizontally—that is, across nations or cultures. Market segmentation identifies individual customers who desire similar benefits and exhibit similar behaviors, and groups them into (relatively) homogeneous segments (where the segments are as dissimilar as possible). Armed with knowledge of customer preferences, the customization versus standardization dilemma is quite easily resolved. It makes sense to customize experiential attributes for customers in market segments who are willing to pay a premium, and standardize (other) service attributes where the costs of customization outweigh the increased contribution margins from customers. So, it is critically important to understand how customers make trade-offs between experiential attributes and price (e.g., using conjoint analysis or other market research techniques). Then, services can be designed, marketed, and delivered with the specific preferences of each target segment in mind. Note that this analysis brings us full circle back to the notion of cocreation: creating excellent customer service experiences (by understanding their preferences) that (in turn) create cash flows for the organization, leading to long-term business success.

Point to Ponder: What challenges do you foresee in applying service principles in emerging economies rather than developed economies?

Future Directions and Challenges

There is now widespread recognition that service creates excellent customer experiences that strengthen bonds between the organization and its customers and thereby increases competitive advantage in the marketplace. After over 30 years of rigorous research, business experts have garnered many insights about how to innovate and improve service to create and enhance relationships and achieve business success. However, since markets change, organizations must be attentive and innovative in creating and delivering service. Consequently, there is much more to learn. This chapter concludes by listing some of the crucial questions currently facing organizations. Two good sources on these crucial questions are the Marketing Science Institute Research Priorities (www.msi.org) and the Journal of Service Research issue on research priorities.[7]

Customer Participation

Coproduction and cocreation is a crucial, but highly variable, component of service design and delivery. Yet, little is known about how managers should understand and plan for customer participation. What is the role of behavioral targeting? How do organizations integrate service-excellent strategies consistently and cost-effectively to enhance customer experiences and build relationships? Moreover, how can organizations create and sustain relationships with customers, recognizing that customers are actively engaged with service brands, employees, and other customers? How should organizations manage relationships when connections are no longer uni-directional (from an organization to customers or potential customers via mass communications) but multidirectional (customized and personalized connections among organizations and customers within a network)? What does this imply for organizations who wish to build brand equity? How can retailers leverage virtual reality, robotics, and other novel ways of interacting with customers?

Innovation

Many organizations have realized lately that they have capabilities for managing innovation in goods or technologies but not for customer experience innovation. How can organizations identify attractive opportunities for innovation, as well as develop and commercialize new services? What are the key elements of a disciplined approach to innovation, including coordinating people, processes, and physical elements to create new solutions for customers? Can these notions be applied to novel customer experiences, such as emerging markets or marketing to economically or socially disadvantaged groups? What design principles apply in these situations? What is the role of aesthetics in designing customer experiences?

Technology

New technologies are disrupting traditional business models. How can incumbent companies proactively identify new market opportunities? How should they respond if competitors encroach from adjacent market spaces? The Internet of Things is revolutionizing many industries. How can organizations integrate these activities to innovate or improve the customer experience? How can organizations respond to disintermediation that arises from technological advances?

Digital Services and Solutions

Rapid advances in information technology have created opportunities for digitized services, raising the following questions:[8] What is the role of usability (in website navigation, digital products, or both)? How should organizations trade-off customization of digital services (through the acquisition and use of customer information) and the creation of trusting relationships with customers (through the provision of privacy and security)? How should organizations integrate a service-centered customer experience approach into traditional manufacturing and technology organizations?

Managing Information Flows

Computer-mediated environments are much different than traditional service environments, with the former characterized by increased information flows, interactivity, reduced information asymmetry between buyers and sellers, and a shift away from geographically based competition. How can organizations address the challenges and opportunities of information rich, real-time service environments? What new capabilities are required for organizations and the people within them? For example, how can organizations leverage customer-initiated communications or customer-to-customer communications? How should managers think about on-demand sharing services? How can organizations better leverage social networks?

Convergence of Media and Service Channels

There has been a proliferation of marketing communications options, fragmentation of media, and convergence of media and service channels. How can organizations coordinate service activities across diverse channels, including personal selling, mass media, direct, Internet, and retail outlets? How can they create synergies between customer–employee interactions and computer-mediated interactions? What are appropriate performance metrics for the effectiveness of communications given that customers use multiple devices and portals? How do organizations standardize service delivery yet retain flexibility in global markets?

Profitable Resource Allocation

What new business models can help guide investments in innovation, service creation and delivery, and customer experience improvement? What are some effective ways of achieving coherency and consistency in service design and delivery—that is, consistency across organizational functions, units, channels, and over time? How do successful organizations allocate resources across channels (i.e., customer touch points) to create effective and efficient experiences for customers? How does an organization successfully function within a dynamic value network, rather than a supply chain?

Customer Portfolio Analysis

Organizations focus on return on investment and the development of metrics that can guide strategic decision making. How can organizations better combine financial metrics with customer metrics? Although scholarly work provides guidance, there are no well-developed software tools for identifying the mix of customers that will optimize the organization return for a given level of risk (or vice versa). Without these tools, managers cannot know how to optimally allocate resources across customers and activities.

A common theme throughout this book is that changes in the business environment are transforming how organizations and customers cocreate experiences that build relationships and generate value for all parties. In a rapidly evolving marketplace, one key tenet is paramount:

Final Thought

A customer-focused, service-centric perspective on creating experiences that build relationships requires organizations to *keep learning—and turn insight into action!*

Notes

1. Karmarkar (2004).
2. Holt, Quelch, and Taylor (2004).
3. Jaworski and Kohli (1993).
4. Burgess and Nyajeka (2007).
5. Agarwal, Malhotra, and Bolton (2010).

6. Bolton and Myers (2003).
7. Ostrom et al. (2015).
8. Bolton (2003).

References

Accenture. 2015. "Digital Business Era: Stretch Your Boundaries." *Accenture Technology Vision.* http://techtrends.accenture.com/us-en/downloads/Accenture_Technology_Vision_2015.pdf (accessed November 14, 2015).

Agarwal, J., N.K. Malhotra, and R.N. Bolton. 2010. "A Cross-National and Cross-Cultural Approach to Global Market Segmentation: An Application Using Consumers' Perceived Service Quality." *Journal of International Marketing* 18, no. 3, pp. 18–40.

Albrecht, K., and L.J. Bradford. 1990. "The Service Advantage." Technical Assistance Research Programs, Inc. (TARP) Report to the White House Office of Consumer Affairs. Homewood, IL: Dow Jones-Irwin.

Anderson, E.W. 1998. "Customer Satisfaction and Word of Mouth." *Journal of Service Research* 1, no. 1, pp. 5–17.

Anderson, E.W., and C. Fornell. 2000. "The Customer Satisfaction Index as a Leading Indicator." *Handbook of Service Marketing and Management,* 255–67. London: Sage Publications.

Anderson, E.W., C. Fornell, and D.R. Lehmann. 1994. "Customer Satisfaction, Market Share, and Profitability: Findings from Sweden." *Journal of Marketing* 58, no. 3, pp. 53–66.

Anderson, E.W., C. Fornell, and R.T. Rust. 1997. "Customer Satisfaction, Productivity, and Profitability: Differences Between Goods and Services." *Marketing Science* 16, no. 2, pp. 129–45.

Anderson, E.W., and M.W. Sullivan. 1993. "The Antecedents and Consequences of Customer Satisfaction for Firms." *Marketing Science* 12, no. 2, pp. 125–43.

Ansari, A., C.F. Mela, and S.A. Neslin. 2008. "Customer Channel Migration." *Journal of Marketing Research* 45, no. 1, pp. 60–76.

Arnold, M.J., and K.E. Reynolds. 2012. "Approach and Avoidance Motivation: Investigating Hedonic Consumption in a Retail Setting." *Journal of Retailing* 88, no. 3, pp. 399–411.

Babin, B.J., W.R. Darden, and M. Griffin. 1994. "Work and/or Fun: Measuring Hedonic and Utilitarian Shopping Value." *Journal of Consumer Research* 20, no. 3, pp. 644–56.

Bagozzi, R.P., and U. Dholakia. 1999. "Goal Setting and Goal Striving in Consumer Behavior." *Journal of Marketing* 63, no. 1, pp. 19–32.

Baker, J., A. Parasuraman, D. Grewal, and G.B. Voss. 2002. "The Influence of Multiple Store Environment Cues on Perceived Merchandise Value Patronage Intentions." *Journal of Marketing* 66, no. 2, pp. 120–41.

Barbaro, M. 2006. "If Preppies Took Over Wal-Mart." *New York Times*, October 3, C1, 6.

Bendapudi, N., and R.P. Leone. 2003. "Psychological Implications of Customer Participation in Co-Production." *Journal of Marketing* 67, no. 1, pp. 14–28.

Berger, P.D., and N.I. Nasr. 1998. "Customer Lifetime Value: Marketing Models and Applications." *Journal of Interactive Marketing* 12, no. 1, pp. 17–30.

Berry, L.L. 1980. "Services Marketing is Different." *Business* 30, no. 3, pp. 24–29.

Berry, L.L. 1981. "The Customer as Employee." *Journal of Retail Banking* 31, no. 1, pp. 33–40.

Berry, L.L. 1983. "Relationship Marketing." In *Emerging Perspectives on Services Marketing*, eds. L.L. Berry, G.L. Shostack, G. Upah, 25–28. Chicago, IL: American Marketing Association.

Berry, L.L., and N. Bendapudi. 2003. "Clueing in Customers." *Harvard Business Review* 81, no. 2, pp. 100–6.

Berry, L.L., K. Seiders, and D. Grewal. 2002. "Understanding Service Convenience." *Journal of Marketing* 66, no. 3, pp. 1–17.

Berry, L.L., V. Shankar, J.T. Parish, S. Cadwallader, and T. Dotzel. 2006. "Creating New Markets Through Service Innovation." *MIT Sloan Management Review* 47, no. 2, pp. 56–63.

Bitner, M.J. 1992. "Servicescapes: The Impact of Physical Surroundings on Customers and Employees." *Journal of Marketing* 56, no. 2, pp. 57–71.

Bitner, M.J. 1993. "Managing the Evidence of Service." In *Service Quality Handbook*, eds. E.E. Scheuing and W.F. Christopher, 358–70. New York: American Marketing Association.

Bitner, M.J. 1995. "Building Service Relationships: It's All About Promises." *Journal of the Academy of Marketing Science* 23, no. 4, pp. 246–51.

Bitner, M.J., B.H. Booms, and M.S. Tetreault. 1990. "The Service Encounter: Diagnosing Favorable and Unfavorable Incidents." *Journal of Marketing* 54, no. 1, pp. 71–84.

Bitner, M.J., S.W. Brown, and M.L. Meuter. 2000. "Technology Infusion in Service Encounters." *Journal of the Academy of Marketing Science* 28, no. 1, pp. 138–49.

Blattberg, R.C., and J. Deighton. 1996. "Manage Marketing by the Customer Equity Test." *Harvard Business Review* 74, no. 4, pp. 136–44.

Blattberg, R.C., G. Getz, and J.S. Thomas. 2001. *Customer Equity: Building and Managing Relationships as Valuable Assets*. Cambridge, MA: Harvard Business Press.

Bock, L. 2015. *Work Rules*. New York: The Hatchette Book Group.

Bolton, R.N. 1998. "A Dynamic Model of the Duration of the Customer's Relationship with a Continuous Service Provider: The Role of Satisfaction." *Marketing Science* 17, no. 1, pp. 45–65.

Bolton, R.N. 2003. "Marketing Challenges of E-Services." *Communications of the Association for Computing Machinery* 46, no. 6, pp. 43–44.

Bolton, L.E., and J.W. Alba. 2006. "Price Fairness: Good and Service Differences and the Role of Vendor Costs." *Journal of Consumer Research* 33, no. 2, pp. 258–65.

Bolton, R.N., and J.H. Drew. 1991a. "A Longitudinal Analysis of the Impact of Service Changes on Customer Attitudes." *Journal of Marketing* 55, no. 1, pp. 1–10.

Bolton, R.N., and J.H. Drew. 1991b. "A Multi-Stage Model of Customers' Assessments of Service Quality and Value." *Journal of Consumer Research* 17, no. 4, pp. 375–84.

Bolton, R.N., and J.H. Drew. 1994. "Linking Customer Satisfaction to Service Operations and Outcomes." In *Service Quality: New Directions in Theory and Practice*, eds. R.T. Rust and R.L. Oliver, 173–200. Newbury Park, CA: Sage Publications.

Bolton, R.N., A. Gustafsson, J. McColl-Kennedy, N.J. Sirianni, and D.K. Tse. 2014. "Small Details that Make Big Differences: A Radical Approach to Consumption Experience as a Firm's Differentiating Strategy." *Journal of Service Management* 25, no. 2, pp. 253–74.

Bolton, R.N., P.K. Kannan, and M.D. Bramlett. 2000. "Implication of Loyalty Programs and Service Experiences for Customer Retention and Value." *Journal of the Academy of Marketing Science* 28, no. 1, pp. 95–108.

Bolton, R.N., and K.N. Lemon. 1999. "A Dynamic Model of Customers' Usage of Services: Usage as an Antecedent of Satisfaction." *Journal of Marketing Research* 36, no. 2, pp. 171–86.

Bolton, R.N., K.N. Lemon, and M.D. Bramlett. 2006. "The Effect of Service Experiences over Time on a Supplier's Retention of Business Customers." *Management Science* 52, no. 12, pp. 1811–23.

Bolton, R.N., K.N. Lemon, and P.C. Verhoef. 2004. "The Theoretical Underpinnings of Customer Asset Management: A Framework and Propositions for Future Research." *Journal of the Academy of Marketing Science* 32, no. 3, pp. 271–92.

Bolton, R.N., K.N. Lemon, and P.C. Verhoef. 2008. "Expanding Business-to-Business Customer Relationships: Modeling the Customer's Upgrade Decision." *Journal of Marketing* 72, no. 1, pp. 46–64.

Bolton, R.N., and M.B. Myers. 2003. "Price-Based Global Market Segmentation for Services." *Journal of Marketing* 67, no. 3, pp. 108–28.

Bolton, R.N., A. Parasuraman, A. Hoefnagels, N. Migchels, S. Kabadayi, T. Gruber, Y.K. Loureiro, and D. Solnet. 2013. "Understanding Gen Y and Their Use of Social Media: A Review and Research Agenda." *Journal of Service Management* 24, no. 3, pp. 245–67.

Bolton, R.N., and S. Saxena-Iyer. 2009. "Interactive Services: A Framework, Synthesis and Research Directions." *Journal of Interactive Marketing* 23, no. 1, pp. 91–104.

Bolton, R.N., A.K. Smith, and J. Wagner. 2003. "Striking the Right Balance: Designing Service to Enhance Business-to-Business Relationships." *Journal of Service Research* 5, no. 4, pp. 271–91.

Bolton, R.N., and C. Tarasi. 2015. "Risk Considerations in the Management of Customer Equity." In *Handbook of Research on Customer Equity in Marketing*, eds. V. Kumar and D. Shah, 335–62. Northampton, MA: Edward Elgar Publishing.

Booz-Allen Hamilton. 2001. "Customer Solutions: Building a Strategically Aligned Business Model." *INSIGHTS* 7, pp. 1–6.

Boulding, W., A. Kalra, R. Staelin, and V.A. Zeithaml. 1993. "A Dynamic Process Model of Service Quality: From Expectations to Behavioral Intentions." *Journal of Marketing Research* 30, no. 1, pp. 7–27.

Bowen, D.E., and B. Schneider. 2014. "A Service Climate Synthesis and Future Research Agenda." *Journal of Service Research* 17, no. 1, pp. 5–22.

Burgess, S.M., and P. Nyajeka. 2007. "Market Orientation and Performance in Low-Income Countries: The Case of Zimbabwean Retailers." *Advances in International Management Journal* 20, pp. 215–57.

Burnham, T.A., J.K. Frels, and V. Mahajan. 2003. "Consumer Switching Costs: A Typology, Antecedents, and Consequences." *Journal of the Academy of Marketing Science* 31, no. 2, pp. 109–26.

Campbell, C.S., P.P. Maglio, and M.M. Davis. 2011. "From Self-Service to Super-Service: A Resource Mapping Framework for Co-Creating Value by Shifting the Boundary Between Provider and Customer." *Information Systems and E-Business Management* 9, no. 2, pp. 173–91.

Campbell, M.C., and C. Warren. 2015. "The Progress Bias in Goal Pursuit: When One Step Forward Seems Larger than One Step Back." *Journal of Consumer Research* 41, no. 5, pp. 1316–31.

Caplan, J. 2006. "Scents and Sensibility." *Time*, October 16, 66–67.

Carlzon, J. 1987. *Moments of Truth*. New York: Harper Perennial.

Chang, K. 2006. "Enlisting Science's Lessons to Entice More Shoppers to Spend More." *New York Times*, September 19, D3.

Chang, W., and S.A. Taylor. January 2016. "The Effectiveness of Customer Participation in New Product Development: A Meta-Analysis." *Journal of Marketing* 80, no. 1, pp. 47–64. doi:10.1509/jm.14.0057

Chase, R.B. 1978. "Where Does the Customer Fit in a Service Operation?" *Harvard Business Review* 56, no. 6, pp. 137–42.

Chesbrough, H., and J. Spohrer. 2006. "A Research Manifesto for Services Science." *Communications of the ACM* 49, no. 7, pp. 35–40.

Colgate, M.R., and P.J. Danaher. 2000. "Implementing a Customer Relationship Strategy: The Asymmetric Impact of Poor Versus Excellent Execution." *Journal of the Academy of Marketing Science* 28, no. 3, pp. 375–87.

Cooil, B., T.L. Keiningham, L. Aksoy, and M. Hsu. 2007. "A Longitudinal Analysis of Customer Satisfaction and Share of Wallet: Investigating the Moderating Effect of Customer Characteristics." *Journal of Marketing* 71, no. 1, pp. 67–83.

Crosby, L.A., and N. Stephens. 1987. "Effects of Relationship Marketing on Satisfaction, Retention, and Prices in the Life Insurance Industry." *Journal of Marketing Research* 24, no. 4, pp. 404–11.

Cunningham, S. 1967. "The Major Dimensions of Perceived Risk." In *Risk Taking and Information Handling in Consumer Behavior*, ed. D. Cox, 82–108. Cambridge, MA: Harvard University Press.

Danaher, P.J., and R.T. Rust. 1996. "Rejoinder: Indirect Financial Benefits from Service Quality." *Quality Management Journal* 3, no. 2.

Daurer, S., D. Molitor, M. Spann, and P. Manchanda. 2015. "Consumer Search Behavior on the Mobile Internet: An Empirical Analysis." Ross School of Business Working Paper No. 1275. http://papers.ssrn.com/sol3/papers.cfm?abstract_id=2603242

De Geus, A.P. 1988. "Planning as Learning." *Harvard Business Review* 62, no. 2, pp. 70–74.

Dell, M. 2001. "When Interviewed for American Way magazine in 2001." *American Way*, October 1.

Dellande, S., M.C. Gilly, and J.L. Graham. 2004. "Gaining Compliance and Losing Weight: The Role of the Service Provider in Health Care Services." *Journal of Marketing* 68, no. 3, pp. 78–91.

Dhar, R., and R. Glazer. 2003. "Hedging Customers." *Harvard Business Review* 81, no. 5, pp. 86–92.

Dong, W., S.D. Swain, and P.D. Berger. 2007. "The Role of Channel Quality in Customer Equity Management." *Journal of Business Research* 60, no. 12, pp. 1243–52.

Elliott Christopher. 2006. "Plush Toys Out. Weary Adults In." *New York Times*, September 26, C10.

Elliott Stuart. 2006. "Letting Consumers Control Marketing: Priceless." *The New York Times*, October 9, C8.

Fombelle, P.W., C.B. Jarvis, J. Ward, and L. Ostrom. 2012. "Leveraging Customers' Multiple Identities: Identity Synergy as a Driver of Organizational Identification." *Journal of the Academy of Marketing Science* 40, no. 4, pp. 587–604.

Fornell, C., M.D. Johnson, E.W. Anderson, J. Cha, and B.E. Bryant. 1996. "The American Customer Satisfaction Index: Nature, Purpose, and Findings." *Journal of Marketing* 60, no. 4, pp. 7–18.

Fornell, C., S. Mithas, F.V. Morgeson III, and M.S. Krishnan. 2006. "Customer Satisfaction and Stock Prices: High Returns, Low Risk." *Journal of Marketing* 70, no. 1, pp. 3–14.

Fornell, C., and B. Wernerfelt. 1987. "Defensive Marketing Strategy by Customer Complaint Management: A Theoretical Analysis." *Journal of Marketing Research* 24, no. 4, pp. 337–46.

Fortune. 2006. "Most Admired Companies." http://money.cnn.com/magazines/fortune/mostadmired/industries/industry_59.html (accessed December 13, 2015).

Frambach, R.T., H.C. Roest, and T.V. Krishnan. 2007. "The Impact of Consumer Internet Experience on Channel Preference and Usage Intentions across the Different Stages of the Buying Process." *Journal of Interactive Marketing* 21, no. 2, pp. 26–41.

Fundin, A., L. Witell, and H. Gebauer. 2012. "Service Transition: Finding the Right Position on the Goods-to-Services Continuum." *International Journal of Modelling in Operations Management* 2, no. 1, pp. 69–88.

Gensler, S., F. Völckner, Y. Liu-Thompkins, and C. Wiertz. 2013. "Managing Brands in the Social Media Environment." *Journal of Interactive Marketing* 27, no. 4, pp. 242–56.

Giebelhausen, M., S.G. Robinson, N.J. Sirianni, and M.K. Brady. 2014. "When Technology Functions as a Barrier or Benefit to Service Encounters." *Journal of Marketing* 78, no. 4, pp. 113–24.

Gilly, M.C., and B.D. Gelb. 1982. "PostPurchase Consumer Processes and the Complaining Consumer." *Journal of Consumer Research* 9, no. 3, pp. 323–28.

Gilly, M.C., and M. Wolfinbarger. 1998. "Advertising's Internal Audience." *Journal of Marketing* 62, no. 1, pp. 69–88.

Goldstein, S.M., R. Johnston, J. Duffy, and J. Rao. 2002. "The Service Concept: The Missing Link in Service Design Research?" *Journal of Operations Management* 20, no. 2, pp. 121–34.

Grőnroos, C. 1984. "A Service Quality Model and Its Marketing Implications." *European Journal of Marketing* 18, no. 4, pp. 36–44.

Grőnroos, C. 1988. "Service Quality: The Six Criteria of Good Perceived Service." *Review of Business* 9, no. 3, p. 10.

Grőnroos, C. 1990. *Service Management and Marketing: Managing the Moments of Truth in Service Competition*. Lexington, MA: Lexington Books.

Grove, S.J., and R.P. Fisk. 1992. "The Service Experience as Theater." *Advances in Consumer Research* 19, no. 1, pp. 455–62.

Gupta, S. 2009. "Customer-Based Valuation." *Journal of Interactive Marketing* 23, no. 2, pp. 169–78.

Gupta, S., D.M. Hanssens, B. Hardie, W. Kahn, V. Kumar, N. Lin, N. Ravishanker, and S. Sriram. 2006. "Modeling Customer Lifetime Value." *Journal of Service Research* 9, no. 2, pp. 139–55.

Gupta, S., D.R. Lehmann, and J.A. Stuart. 2004. "Valuing Customers." *Journal of Marketing Research* 41, no. 1, pp. 7–18.

Gupta, S., and D.R. Lehmann. 2005. *Managing Customers as Investments. The Strategic Value of Customers in the Long Run*. Upper Saddle River, NJ: Wharton School Publishing.

Hagtvedt, H., and V.M. Patrick. 2014. "Consumer Response to Overstyling: Balancing Aesthetics and Functionality in Product Design." *Psychology and Marketing* 31, no. 7, pp. 518–25.

Hardekopf, B. 2015. "The Big Data Breaches of 2014." *Forbes*, January 13.

Henkoff, R. 1994. "Service is Everybody's Business." *Fortune*, 129, no. 13, pp. 48–50.

Heshmati, A. 2003. "Productivity Growth, Efficiency and Outsourcing in Manufacturing and Service Industries." *Journal of Economic Surveys* 17, no. 1, pp. 79–112.

Heskett, J.L., and L.A. Schlesinger. 1994. "Putting the Service-Profit Chain to Work." *Harvard Business Review* 72, no. 2, pp. 164–74.

Hoffman, D.L., and M. Fodor. 2010. "Can You Measure the ROI of your Social Media Marketing?" *MIT Sloan Management Review* 52, no. 1, pp. 41–49.

Hoffman, D.L., and T.P. Novak. January 17, 2012. "Why Do People Use Social Media? Empirical Findings and a New Theoretical Framework for Social Media Goal Pursuit." http://papers.ssrn.com/sol3/papers.cfm?abstract_id=1989586

Holt, D.B., J.A. Quelch, and E.L. Taylor. 2004. "How Global Brands Compete." *Harvard Business Review* 82, no. 9, pp. 68–75.

Hsieh, T. 2010. "How I Did It: Zappos's CEO on Going to Extremes for Customers." *Harvard Business Review* 88, no. 7, pp. 41–45.

Hui, M.K., and J.E.G. Bateson. 1991. "Perceived Control and the Effects of Crowding and Consumer Choice on the Service Experience." *Journal of Consumer Research* 18, no. 2, pp. 174–84.

Hui, S.K., E.T. Bradlow, and P.S. Fader. 2009. "Testing Behavioral Hypotheses Using an Integrated Model of Grocery Store Shopping Path and Purchase Behavior." *Journal of Consumer Research* 36, no. 3, pp. 478–93.

Izard, C.E. 1991. *The Psychology of Emotions*. New York: Springer Science & Business Media.

Jackson, C., and P. Sanders. 2006. "The New Hotel Name Game." *New York Times*, September 9–10, P1, P6.

Jaworski, B.J., and A.K. Kohli. 1993. "Market Orientation: Antecedents and Consequences." *Journal of Marketing* 57, no. 3, pp. 53–70.

Johnson, M.D., and F. Selnes. 2004. "Customer Portfolio Management: Toward a Dynamic Theory of Exchange Relationships." *Journal of Marketing* 68, no. 2, pp. 1–17.

Jones, M.A., D.L. Mothersbaugh, and S.E. Beatty. 2002. "Why Customers Stay: Measuring the Underlying Dimensions of Services Switching Costs and Managing Their Differential Strategic Outcomes." *Journal of Business Research* 55, no. 6, pp. 441–50.

Kamakura, W.A., M. Wedel, F. De Rosa, and J.A. Masson. 2003. "Cross-Selling Through Database Marketing: A Mixed Data Factor Analyzer for Data Augmentation and Prediction." *International Journal of Research in Marketing* 20, no. 1, pp. 45–65.

Kaplan, R., and D. Norton. 2005. "The Balanced Scorecard—Measures that Drive Performance." *Harvard Business Review* 84, no. 3, pp. 100–9.

Karmarkar, U. 2004. "Will You Survive the Services Revolution?" *Harvard Business Review* 82, no. 6, pp. 100–7.

Keane, T.J., and P. Wang. 1995. "Applications for the Lifetime Value Model in Modern Newspaper Publishing." *Journal of Direct Marketing* 9, no. 2, pp. 59–66.

Keaveney, S.M. 1995. "Customer Switching Behavior in Service Industries: An Exploratory Study." *Journal of Marketing* 59, no. 2, pp. 71–82.

Keller, K.L. 1993. "Conceptualizing, Measuring, and Managing Customer-Based Brand Equity." *Journal of Marketing* 57, no. 1, pp. 1–22.

Keller, K.L. 2000. "The Brand Report Card." *Harvard Business Review* 78, no. 1, pp. 147–58.

Kordupleski, R.E., R.T. Rust, and A.J. Zahorik. 1993. "Why Improving Quality Doesn't Improve Quality. Or Whatever Happened to Marketing?" *California Management Review* 35, no. 3, pp. 82–95.

Kumar, P. 1999. "The Impact of Long-Term Client Relationships on the Performance of Business Service Firms." *Journal of Service Research* 2, no. 1, pp. 4–18.

Kumar, V., and R. Venkatesan. 2005. "Who Are the Multichannel Shoppers and How Do They Perform?: Correlates of Multichannel Shopping Behavior." *Journal of Interactive Marketing* 19, no. 2, pp. 44–62.

LaValle, S. 2015. "Business Analytics and Optimization for the Intelligent Enterprise." IBM Institute for Business Value. www-03.ibm.com/innovation/us/smarterplanet/assets/smarterBusiness/business_analytics/gbe03211-usen-00.pdf (accessed August 11, 2015)

Lee, R.P., and R. Grewal. 2004. "Strategic Responses to New Technologies and Their Impact on Firm Performance." *Journal of Marketing* 68, no. 4, pp. 157–71.

Limin, C. 2012. "Succession Proves to be a Headache at Alibaba Group." *China Daily News*, August 20, 2012.

Logue, A.C. 2006. "Swisscom's Team of Special Customer Service Agents Create a Competitive Advantage." Oracle Report. www.oracle.com/us/corporate/profit/features/p46communications-143698.html

Lohr, S. 2015. "IBM's Design-Centered Strategy to Set Free the Squares." *New York Times*, November 15.

Lovelock, C.H. 1983. "Classifying Services to Gain Strategic Marketing Insights." *Journal of Marketing* 47, no. 3, pp. 9–20.

Lovelock, C.H. 1992. *Managing Services: Marketing, Operations and Human Resources*, Englewood Cliffs, NJ: Prentice-Hall.

Lovelock, C.H., and R.F. Young. 1979. "Look to Consumers to Increase Productivity." *Harvard Business Review* 57, no. 3, pp. 168–78.

Loveman, G.W. 1998. "Employee Satisfaction, Customer Loyalty, and Financial Performance: An Empirical Examination of the Service Profit Chain in Retail Banking." *Journal of Service Research* 1, no. 1, pp. 18–31.

Lovett, M.J., R. Peres, and R. Shachar. 2013. "On Brands and Word of Mouth." *Journal of Marketing Research* 50, no. 4, pp. 427–44.

Lusch, R.F., S.L. Vargo, and M. O'Brien. 2007. "Competing Through Service: Insights from Service-Dominant Logic." *Journal of Retailing* 83, no. 1, pp. 5–18.

Manchanda, P., G. Packard, and A. Pattabhiramaia. 2012. "Social Dollars: The Economic Impact of Customer Participation in a Firm-Sponsored Online Community." Marketing Science Institute Working Paper, Cambridge, MA. http://papers.ssrn.com/sol3/papers.cfm?abstract_id=1984350

Magrath, A.J. 1986. "When Marketing Services, 4 Ps Are Not Enough." *Business Horizons* 29, no. 3, pp. 44–50.

McAlexander, J.H., J.W. Schouten, and H.F. Koenig. 2002. "Building Brand Community." *Journal of Marketing* 66, no. 1, pp. 38–64.

Mende, M., R.N. Bolton, and M.J. Bitner. 2013. "Decoding Customer–Firm Relationships: How Attachment Styles Help Explain Customers' Preferences for Closeness, Repurchase Intentions, and Changes in Relationship Breadth." *Journal of Marketing Research* 50, no. 1, pp. 125–42.

Meuter, M.L., M.J. Bitner, A.L. Ostrom, and S.W. Brown. 2005. "Choosing Among Alternative Service Delivery Modes: An Investigation of Customer Trial of Self-Service Technologies." *Journal of Marketing* 69, no. 2, pp. 61–83.

Meuter, M.L., A.L. Ostrom, R.I. Roundtree, M.J. Bitner. 2000. "Self-Service Technologies: Understanding Customer Satisfaction with Technology-Based Service Encounters." *Journal of Marketing* 64, no. 3, pp. 50–64.

Michon, R., J.C. Chebat, and L.W. Turley. 2005. "Mall Atmospherics: the Interaction Effects of the Mall Environment on Shopping Behavior." *Journal of Business Research* 58, no. 5, pp. 576–83.

Mizik, N., and R. Jacobson. 2008. "The Financial Value Impact of Perceptual Brand Attributes." *Journal of Marketing Research* 45, pp. 115–32.

Montoya-Weiss, M.M., G.B. Voss, and D. Grewal. 2003. "Determinants of Online Channel Use and Overall Satisfaction with a Relational, Multichannel Service Provider." *Journal of the Academy of Marketing Science* 31, no. 4, pp. 448–58.

Moon, Y., and J.A. Quelch. 2003. *Starbucks: Delivering Customer Service.* Watertown, MA: Harvard Business School Publishing.

Morgan, R.M., and S.D. Hunt. 1994. "The Commitment-Trust Theory of Relationship Marketing." *Journal of Marketing* 58, no. 3, pp. 20–38.

Morwitz, V.G., and D. Schmittlein. 1992. "Using Segmentation to Improve Sales Forecasts Based on Purchase Intent: Which "Intenders" Actually Buy?" *Journal of Marketing Research* 29, no. 4, pp. 391–405.

Narver, J.C., and S.F. Slater. 1990. "The Effect of a Market Orientation on Business Profitability." *Journal of Marketing* 54, no. 4, pp. 20–35.

Neslin, S.A., D. Grewal, R. Leghorn, V. Shankar, M.L. Teerling, J.S. Thomas, and P.C. Verhoef. 2006. "Challenges and Opportunities in Multichannel Customer Management." *Journal of Service Research* 9, no. 2, pp. 95–112.

Neslin, S.A., and V. Shankar. 2009. "Key Issues in Multichannel Customer Management: Current Knowledge and Future Directions." *Journal of Interactive Marketing* 23, no. 1, pp. 70–81.

Nitzan, I., and B. Libai. 2011. "Social Effects on Customer Retention." *Journal of Marketing* 75, no. 6, pp. 24–38.

Noble, S.M., D.A. Griffith, and M.G. Weinberger. 2005. "Consumer Derived Utilitarian Value and Channel Utilization in a Multichannel Retail Context." *Journal of Business Research* 58, no. 12, pp. 1643–51.

Nyer, P.U. 1997. "A Study of the Relationships Between Cognitive Appraisals and Consumption Emotions." *Journal of the Academy of Marketing Science* 25, no. 4, pp. 296–304.

Oliver, R.L. 1993. "Cognitive, Affective, and Attribute bases of the Satisfaction Response." *Journal of Consumer Research*, pp. 418–30.

Oliver, R.L. 1999. "Whence Consumer Loyalty?" *Journal of Marketing* 63, no. 4, pp. 33–44.

Oliver, R.L. 2015. *Satisfaction: A Behavioral Perspective on the Consumer.* New York: Routledge.

Oliver, R.L., and J.E. Swan. 1989. "Consumer Perceptions of Interpersonal Equity and Satisfaction in Transactions: A Field Survey Approach." *Journal of Marketing* 53, no. 2, pp. 21–35.

Ostrom, A.L., A. Parasuraman, D.E. Bowen, L. Patrício, C.A. Voss, and K. Lemon. 2015. "Service Research Priorities in a Rapidly Changing Context." *Journal of Sgervice Research* 18, no. 2, pp. 127–59.

Palmatier, R.W., L.K. Scheer, M.B. Houston, K.R. Evans, and S. Gopalakrishna. 2007. "Use of Relationship Marketing Programs in Building Customer–Salesperson and Customer–Firm Relationships: Differential Influences on Financial Outcomes." *International Journal of Research in Marketing* 24, no. 3, pp. 210–23.

Parasuraman, A., V.A. Zeithaml, and L.L. Berry. 1985a. "A Conceptual Model of Service Quality and Its Implications for Further Research." *Journal of Marketing* 49, no. 4, pp. 41–50.

Parasuraman, A., V.A. Zeithaml, and L.L. Berry. 1985b. "Problems and Strategies in Services Marketing." *Journal of Marketing* 49, no. 2, pp. 33–46.

Parasuraman, A., V.A. Zeithaml, and L.L. Berry. 1988. "Servqual: A Multiple-Item Scale for Measuring Consumer Perceptions of Service Quality." *Journal of Retailing* 64, no. 1, pp. 12–40.

Patrick, V.M., and H. Hagtvedt. 2011. "Aesthetic Incongruity Resolution." *Journal of Marketing Research* 48, no. 2, pp. 393–402.

Payne, A., and P. Frow. 2005. "A Strategic Framework for Customer Relationship Management." *Journal of Marketing* 69, no. 4, pp. 167–76.

Payne, A., and J. Rickard. 1997. "Relationship Marketing, Customer Retention and Firm Profitability." Working Paper Cranfield School of Management, UK.

Peres, R., E. Muller, and V. Mahajan. 2010. "Innovation Diffusion and New Product Growth Models: A Critical Review and Research Directions." *International Journal of Research in Marketing* 27, no. 2, pp. 91–106.

Prahalad, C.K. 2004. "The Cocreation of Value." *Journal of Marketing* 68, no. 1, p. 23.

Prahalad, C.K., and V. Ramaswamy. 2000. "Co-Opting Customer Competence." *Harvard Business Review* 78, no. 1, pp. 79–90.

Ratneshwar, S., L.W. Barsalou, C. Pechmann, and M. Moore. 2001. "Goal-Derived Categories: The Role of Personal and Situational Goals in Category Representations." *Journal of Consumer Psychology* 10, no. 3, pp. 147–57.

Reichheld, F.F. 1992. "Loyalty-Based Management." *Harvard Business Review* 71, no. 2, pp. 64–73.

Reichheld, F.F. 1996. *The Loyalty Effect.* Boston, MA: Harvard Business School Press.

Reichheld, F.R., and W.E. Sasser. 1990. "Zero Defections: Quality Comes to Services." *Harvard Business Review* 68, no. 5, pp. 105–11.

Reichheld, F.R., and T. Teal. 2001. *The Loyalty Effect: The Hidden Force Behind Growth, Profits, and Lasting Value.* Cambridge, MA: Harvard Business Press.

Reinartz, W., and V. Kumar. 2002. "The Mismanagement of Customer Loyalty." *Harvard Business Review* 80, no. 7, pp. 86–95.

Reinartz, W., J.S. Thomas, and V. Kumar. 2005. "Balancing Acquisition and Retention Resources to Maximize Customer Profitability." *Journal of Marketing* 69, no. 1, pp. 63–79.

Richins, M.L. 1997. "Measuring Emotions in the Consumption Experience." *Journal of Consumer Research* 24, no. 2, pp. 127–46.

Roberts, D., and L.Y. Chen. 2015. "China's Hunt for Growth in the Countryside." *Businessweek*, August 27.

Rucci, A.J., S.P. Kirn, and R.T. Quinn. 1998. "The Employee-Customer-Profit Chain at Sears." *Harvard Business Review* 76, no. 1, pp. 82–98.

Rust, R.T., K.N. Lemon, and V.A. Zeithaml. 2004. "Return on Marketing: Using Customer Equity to Focus Marketing Strategy." *Journal of Marketing* 68, no. 1, pp. 109–27.

Rust, R.T., and R.L. Oliver. 1993. *Service Quality: New Directions in Theory and Practice*. Thousand Oak, CA: Sage Publications.

Rust, R.T., and A.J. Zahorik. 1993. "Customer Satisfaction, Customer Retention, and Market Share." *Journal of Retailing* 69, no. 2, pp. 193–215.

Rust, R.T., A.J. Zahorik, and T.L. Keiningham. 1995. "Return on Quality (ROQ): Making Service Quality Financially Accountable." *Journal of Marketing* 59, no. 2, pp. 58–70.

Saran, C. 2015. "What Is Big Data and How Can It Be Used to Competitive Advantage?" *Computer Weekly*. www.computerweekly.com/feature/What-is-big-data-and-how-can-it-be-used-to-gain-competitive-advantage (accessed August 11, 2015).

Schneider, B. 1986. "Notes on Climate and Culture." In *Creativity in Services Marketing: What's New, What Works, What's Developing*, eds. M. Venkatesan, D.M. Schmalensee and C Marshall, 53–67. Chicago, IL: American Marketing Association.

Schneider, B., and D. Bowen. 1985. "Employee and Customer Perceptions of Service in Banks: Replication and Extension." *Journal of Applied Psychology* 70, pp. 423–33.

Schneider, B., and D.E. Bowen. 1993. "The Service Organization: Human Resources Management Is Crucial." *Organizational Dynamics* 21, no. 4, pp. 39–52.

Schneider, B., and D.E. Bowen. 2010. *Winning the Service Game*. New York: Springer.

Schultz, H., and J. Gordon. 2011. *Onward: How Starbucks Fought for Its Life Without Losing Its Soul*. New York: Rodale, Inc.

Seiders, K., G.B. Voss, D. Grewal, and A.L. Godfrey. 2005. "Do Satisfied Customers Buy More? Examining Moderating Influences in a Retailing Context." *Journal of Marketing* 69, no. 4, pp. 26–43.

Sen, S., and C.B. Bhattacharya. 2001. "Does Doing Good Always Lead to Doing Better? Consumer Reactions to Corporate Social Responsibility." *Journal of Marketing Research* 38, no. 2, pp. 225–43.

Shankar, V., L.L. Berry, and T. Dotzel. 2009. "A Practical Guide to Combining Products and Services." *Harvard Business Review* 87, no. 11, pp. 94–99.

Sharkey, J. 2006. "Gun or Bug Spray Not Needed, But You Do Make Your Own Bed." *New York Times*, September 26, C10.

Shostack, G.L. 1984. "Designing Services that Deliver." *Harvard Business Review* 17, no. 1, pp. 133–39.

Sirianni, N.J., M.J. Bitner, S.W. Brown, and N. Mandel. 2013. "Branded Service Encounters: Strategically Aligning Employee Behavior with the Brand Positioning." *Journal of Marketing* 77, no. 6, pp. 108–23.

Smith, A.K., and R.N. Bolton. 1998. "An Experimental Investigation of Service Failure and Recovery: Paradox or Peril?" *Journal of Service Research* 1, no. 1, pp. 65–81.

Smith, A.K., R.N. Bolton, and J. Wagner. 1999. "A Model of Customer Satisfaction With Service Encounters Involving Failure and Recovery." *Journal of Marketing Research* 36, no. 3, pp. 356–72.

Solnet, D., and A. Hood. 2008. "Generation Y as Hospitality Employees: Framing a Research Agenda." *Journal of Hospitality and Tourism Management* 15, no. 1, pp. 59–68.

Solnet, D., and A. Hood. 2010. ""Gen-Gagement": Generational Differences in Employee Enagagement." In *20th Annual Council for Australian University Tourism and Hospitality Education. (CAUTHE) Conference*, pp. 1–11. Australia: University of Tasmania.

Spangenberg, E.R., A.E. Crowley, and P.W. Henderson. 1996. "Improving the Store Environment: Do Olfactory Cues Affect Evaluations and Behaviors?" *Journal of Marketing* 60, no. 2, pp. 67–80.

Srivastava, R.K., T.A. Shervani, and L. Fahey. 1998. "Market-Based Assets and Shareholder Value: A Framework for Analysis." *Journal of Marketing* 62, no. 1, pp. 2–18.

Steel, E. 2015. "Media Earnings Results Are Awaited, a Bit Warily." *New York Times*, November 3.

Szymanski, D.M., and R.T. Hise. 2000. "E-Satisfaction: An Initial Examination." *Journal of Retailing* 76, no. 3, pp. 309–23.

Tarasi, C.O., R.N. Bolton, A. Gustafsson, and B.A. Walker. 2013. "Relationship Characteristics and Cash Flow Variability Implications for Satisfaction, Loyalty, and Customer Portfolio Management." *Journal of Service Research* 16, no. 2, pp. 121–37.

Tarasi, C.O., R.N. Bolton, A. Gustafsson, and L. Witell. 2015. "A Global Study of How Goals and Emotions Influence Consumers' Satisfaction with Their Experience Within and Across Retail Channels." Working Paper, Central Michigan University.

Tarasi, C.O., R.N. Bolton, M.D. Hutt, and B.A. Walker. 2011. "Balancing Risk and Return in a Customer Portfolio." *Journal of Marketing* 75, no. 3, pp. 1–17.

Thomas, J.S., W. Reinartz, and V. Kumar. 2004. "Getting the Most Out of All Your Customers." *Harvard Business Review* 82, no. 7–8, pp. 116–23.

Trusov, M., R.E. Bucklin, and K. Pauwels. 2009. "Effects of Word-of-Mouth Versus Traditional Marketing: Findings from an Internet Social Networking Site." *Journal of Marketing* 73, no. 5, pp. 90–102.

Urban, G.L., and J.R. Hauser. 1993. *Design and Marketing of New Products*. New York: Prentice Hall.

Van Birgelen, M., A. De Jong, and K. De Ruyter. 2006. "Multi-Channel Service Retailing: The Effects of Channel Performance Satisfaction on Behavioral Intentions." *Journal of Retailing* 82, no. 4, pp. 267–77.

Van Doorn, J., K.N. Lemon, V. Mittal, S. Nass, D. Pick, P. Pirner, and P.C. Verhoef. 2010. "Customer Engagement Behavior: Theoretical Foundations and Research Directions." *Journal of Service Research* 13, no. 3, pp. 253–66.

Vargo, S.L., and R.F. Lusch. 2004. "Evolving to a New Dominant Logic for Marketing." *Journal of Marketing* 68, no. 1, pp. 1–17.

Vargo, S.L., and R.F. Lusch. 2008. "Service-Dominant Logic: Continuing the Evolution." *Journal of the Academy of Marketing Science* 36, no. 1, pp. 1–10.

Venkatesan, R., and V. Kumar. 2004. "A Customer Lifetime Value Framework for Customer Selection and Resource Allocation Strategy." *Journal of Marketing* 68, no. 4, pp. 106–25.

Verhoef, P.C. 2003. "Understanding the Effect of Customer Relationship Management Efforts on Customer Retention and Customer Share Development." *Journal of Marketing* 67, no. 4, pp. 30–45.

Verhoef, P.C., P.H. Franses, and J.C. Hoekstra. 2002. "The Effect of Relational Constructs on Customer Referrals and Number of Services Purchased from a Multiservice Provider: Does Age of Relationship Matter?" *Journal of the Academy of Marketing Science* 30, no. 3, pp. 202–16.

Verhoef, P.C., P.K. Kannan, and J.J. Inman. 2015. "From Multi-Channel Retailing to Omni-Channel Retailing: Introduction to the Special Issue on Multi-Channel Retailing." *Journal of Retailing* 91, no. 2, pp. 174–81.

Wang, Y.J., M.S. Minor, and J. Wei. 2011. "Aesthetics and the Online Shopping Environment: Understanding Consumer Responses." *Journal of Retailing* 87, no. 1, pp. 46–58.

Wang, S., and E. Pfanner. 2013. "China's One-Day Shopping Spree Sets Record in Online Sales." *The New York Times*, November 12.

Westbrook, R.A., and R.L. Oliver. 1991. "The Dimensionality of Consumption Emotion Patterns and Consumer Satisfaction." *Journal of Consumer Research* 18, no. 1, pp. 84–91.

Williamson, P.J., and E. Yin. 2014. "Accelerated Innovation: The New Challenge from China." *The Sloan Management Review* 55, no. 4, pp. 27–34.

Wolfinbarger, M., and M.C. Gilly. 2001. "Shopping Online for Freedom, Control, and Fun." *California Management Review* 43, no. 2, pp. 34–55.

Zeithaml, V.A. 1988. "Consumer Perceptions of Price, Quality, and Value: A Conceptual Model and Synthesis of Research." *Journal of Marketing* 52, no. 3, pp. 2–22.

Zeithaml, V.A., and M.J. Bitner. 2000. *Services Marketing: Integrating Customer Focus Across the Firm*. 2nd ed. New York: Irwin McGraw-Hill.

Zeithaml, V.A., R.N. Bolton, J. Deighton, T.L. Keiningham, K.N. Lemon, and J.A. Petersen. 2006. "Forward-Looking Focus: Can Firms Have Adaptive Foresight?" *Journal of Service Research* 9, no. 2, pp. 168–83.

Zeithaml, V.A., S.W. Brown, M.J. Bitner, and J. Salas. 2015. *Profiting From Services and Solutions: What Product-Centric Firms Need to Know.* New York: Business Expert Press.

Zeithaml, V.A., A. Parasuraman, and L.L. Berry. 1985. "Problems and Strategies in Services Marketing." *Journal of Marketing* 49, no. 4, pp. 41–50.

Zeithaml, V.A., A. Parasuraman, and L.L. Berry. 1990. *Delivering Quality Service: Balancing Customer Perceptions and Expectations.* New York: The Free Press.

Zeithaml, V.A., A. Parasuraman, and A. Malhotra. 2000. "Conceptual Framework for Understanding e-Service Quality: Implications for Future Research and Managerial Practice." Marketing Science Institute. Cambridge, MA.

Index

OTHER TITLES IN OUR MARKETING STRATEGY COLLECTION

Naresh Malhotra, Georgia Tech, Editor

- *Developing Successful Marketing Strategies* by Gary W. Randazzo
- *Marketing and Management Models: A Guide to Understanding and Using Business Models* by Yvonne Helen Strong
- *Effective Advertising Strategies for Your Business* by Cong Li
- *Surprise!: The Secret to Customer Loyalty in the Service Sector* by Vincent P. Magnini
- *Sales Promotion Decision Making: Concepts, Principles, and Practice* by Steve Ogden-Barnes and Stella Minahan
- *Smart Marketing: How to Dramatically Grow Your Revenue* by Ahmed Al Akber
- *Market Sensing Today* by Melvin Prince and Constantinos-Vasilios Priporas
- *Launching New Products: Best Marketing and Sales Practices* by John Westman and Paul Sowyrda
- *Marketing Plan Templates for Enhancing Profits* by Elizabeth Rush Kruger

CPSIA information can be obtained
at www.ICGtesting.com
Printed in the USA
FSHW010947290919
62401FS

9 781631 573712